"We live in such a complicated world, to survive. Jane Jackson makes it very c to be aiming to thrive, especially wher very broad and complex concept and ma relevant. A great book for those wanting a richer life."

Andrew Griffiths,
Australia's #1 Small Business and
Entrepreneurial Author

"Jane Jackson's Navigating Career Crossroads is a valuable resource to focus your career planning. Not only are the steps clear but also the techniques to follow as you progress through the steps. The book has wide application for anyone considering what next for their career. Practical and down to earth, by working through the book you will get valuable insights into how to achieve your dream job. I have thoroughly enjoyed the book and feel confident and excited about making the dream job a reality for me."

Sue Seymour,
Capability Development Manager,
Capital & Coast District Health Board

"*Navigating Career Crossroads* is a must read if you're at a turning point in your career. The message is very clear – to market yourself successfully you must understand what you have to offer and what your ideal role looks like and then be resilient, determined and courageous in your search. This excellent book will guide you every step of the way. Apply these principles and you will succeed."

Brian Quirke,
Director, PHR Consulting

"Finding a dream job is hard, it is even harder to switch from one job to the other. This book provides a lot of useful information to guide the reader through this interesting, but frightening process. It will answer a lot of your questions and reduce your stress when trying to land a dream job!"

Cynthia Dearin,
International Business Strategist,
Dearin & Associates

"This book clearly explains the job search strategies that work and shows you how to leverage them to your advantage to make a career change. This is a must read for professionals at all levels!"

Professor Sattar Bawany,
CEO and Master Executive Coach, CEE Global (Centre for Executive Education)

"Highly recommended for everyone who genuinely cares about their careers. *Navigating Career Crossroads* is the perfect way to provide your career journey with the necessary tools and structure to guarantee success."

John Hannelly,

"Everything you need to know to gain clarity about your career direction and successfully secure your ideal role. Highly recommended."

Peter Tobin,
Managing Director,
Worklife International Pty Limited

"Interviews with Jane are always a pleasure, with her extensive experience in career coaching, mixed with compassion and a vibrant can-do attitude. This book makes it possible for you to take control of your career with clarity and focus. A must read to point you in the right direction!"

SteveO,
Sydney FM Broadcaster and Radio Host,
steveoshow.com

"Having worked closely with Jane Jackson for a number of years in career transition coaching, I can vouch for her knowledge, experience and caring manner that is applied to each and every client to assist them deal with a crossroads in their career. Jane applies her own personal transition experiences for the benefit of her clients in this uncertain world in which we are now living. I hope you will enjoy this book and gain new strategies and insights to help manage your own career crossroads."

Peter Black,
Business and Executive Coach, Sydney, Australia,
peterblackcoaching.com

NAVIGATING CAREER CROSSROADS

How to ~~survive~~ thrive when changing direction

JANE JACKSON

© 2020 Jane Jackson

Disclaimer

The material in this publication is of the nature of general comment only, and does not represent professional advice. It is not intended to provide specific guidance for particular circumstances and it should not be relied on as the basis for any decision to take action or not take action on any matter which it covers. Readers should obtain professional advice where appropriate, before making any such decision. The author and publisher disclaim all responsibility and liability to any person, arising directly or indirectly from any person taking or not taking action based on the information in this publication.

The moral right of the author has been asserted.

All rights reserved. Without limiting the rights under copyright restricted above, no part of this publication may be reproduced, stored in or introduced into a retrieval system, or transmitted, in any form or by any means (electronic, mechanical, photocopying, recording or otherwise), without the prior written permission of both the copyright owner and the above publisher of this book.

National Library of Australia Cataloguing-in-Publication entry

Creator: Jackson, Jane, author.

Title: Navigating career crossroads: how to thrive when changing direction / Jane Jackson.

ISBN: 9780648479062

Notes: Includes index.

Subjects: Career changes. Career development. Job search.

Dewey Number: 650.14
Cover illustration: Shutterstock Cover design: Helen Christie
Published by The OMNE Group www.omne.com.au

Dedicated to Mum, Dad, Jess, Jo, Tony and Tommy

Author's Note

Throughout this book I have shared the experiences and insights of many of my clients and colleagues. To protect the privacy of those by request, I have changed their names and other identifying features.

ABOUT THE AUTHOR

Jane Jackson is a career management coach, speaker, LinkedIn trainer and host of YOUR CAREER Podcast. She has over 19 years experience helping thousands of executives across Asia Pacific and Europe, to make a successful career transition, build their personal brands to attract the job opportunities they deserve.

Jane's personal journey and professional transitions have developed her resilience, confidence and clarity enabling her to become a specialist in transition coaching and successfully coach executives from all industries to discover their true passion and career direction.

Jane passionately delivers her 7 Step CAREERS program that enables you to confidently take control, make a change and achieve your career goals.

Jane is an engaging speaker and trainer and enjoys presenting group workshops on Career Management, Personal Branding, Job Search Strategies, Networking, Confidence Building, Wellness in the Workplace, and Stress Management.

Jane's corporate clients include the Reserve Bank of Australia, NSW Police Force, NSW Police Legacy, Cricket NSW, Rio Tinto, Credit Suisse, Australian Graduate School of Management and Chicago Booth Graduate School of Management.

Jane has been the resident career coach on 2UE's Talking Lifestyle Second Career and on Northside Radio's SteveO Show, as Sydney's leading career and life coach. She has appeared on Sky News Business, Huffington Post, Sydney Morning Herald and more.

Download Jane's career resources at www.janejacksoncoach.com, join The Careers Academy at www.thecareersacademy.online, and be inspired by the successful transitions made by her guests on YOUR CAREER Podcast at www.janejacksoncoach.com/podcast

CONTENTS

Introduction 1

The risk of a crisis of confidence 4
How to survive an unexpected career change 6

C **Confidently manage change** 11

The impact of stress on your confidence 13
The key to confidence – understanding change 17
Managing stress 17

A **Assess what makes you tick** 33

1. Your life inventory 36
2. Be clear on your values 44
3. Motivators/demotivators 48
4. Skills and knowledge identification 49
5. Your dream role 54
6. Achievements 56

R **Resumes and your marketing communications** 61

Verbal pitch 62
The 60- to 90-second introduction 62
Verbal pitch template 65
Written marketing material – your resume and cover letters 68
Providing referees 79
LinkedIn and online branding 82
How to ensure your profile is optimised
for search 93
How to use LinkedIn for research 95
How to use LinkedIn for job applications 97

E **EXPRESS YOUR PERSONAL BRAND AND PROFESSIONAL IMAGE**..99

    Your assumed image..103
    Your visual image..104
    Your experienced image 111
    Your proven image 112

E **Explore job search strategies that work** 115

    1. How to use online job boards effectively.....................117
    2. Working with recruitment consultants........................122
    3. Networking..130
    4. Approaching employers directly.................................141
    5. Internships 142
    6. Volunteering...144

R **RELATE YOUR SUITABILITY AT INTERVIEWS** 147

    Interview preparation..148
    What to do during the interview 159
    What types of interviews might you encounter?............165
    What to do after the interview 171
    What will tip the balance for you in an interview? 175

S **Success strategies in your new role**.....................................177

    Determine your needs..178
    Know what you are worth 179
    How to open negotiations..181
    On-boarding into the new role.....................................183

CONCLUSION 187

RESOURCES 189

WITH GRATITUDE..191

INTRODUCTION

"You can't stop the waves, but you can learn to surf."

Jon Kabat-Zinn

Change can be pretty scary.

Whether we're dissatisfied with our job, facing a redundancy or an organisational restructure, career challenges are inevitable. Yet when they hit they can leave us confused, anxious, fearful and stressed. This emotional roller coaster can erode our self-confidence and create confusion about what to do next.

So many of us try to control everything in our lives, including our careers, relationships, finances, physical environment and even our level of happiness! But, with all of this control, what happens to our ability to cope when a major change affects every aspect of our life?

Losing a job is one such change. In fact, losing a job is one of the most stressful events that can happen to us, only ranking below other major life-changing events such as death, divorce, personal illness or major injury.

I'd go so far as to say job losses are causing even more stress today, with a range of additional pressures meaning that a steady job, or steady income, is more important than ever before.

As the cost of living continues to rise, more and more couples need two incomes to cover their expenses, meaning that being out of work places significant strain on your finances.

Additionally, finding a new job can be even more of a challenge today, with greater competition as more degree-qualified Gen Ys and Millennials enter the job market, more baby boomers take longer to retire, and more jobs are farmed off-shore. This means that, once you're out of a job, it may be months before you find something new, adding more strain to your finances, relationships and health.

And because our careers have a greater impact on our lives than ever before, it's very unusual for any of us to go through a career transition without experiencing several other challenges in our lives as well. I know many clients and friends who have experienced a job loss or redundancy and, at the same time, have also had to deal with the stress of a marital separation or divorce, or had recently become parents, or had seriously ill relatives to take care of while looking for a new role.

No matter how much we try to plan for smooth sailing, all of us know that change is inevitable. In fact, as the Greek philosopher Heraclitus (535BC–475BC) said, "Nothing endures but change. Change is the only constant. "

So if we know that change is inevitable, in our careers and in our lives, why do so many of us struggle with it?

Through discussions with over 8,000 clients over the past 19 years, I've found that there are three main reasons we experience resistance and reluctance to accept change, and feel so uncomfortable when it happens.

1. Fear of the unknown

This type of resistance occurs when things happen without advance warning. When change (especially what is perceived as negative change) is pushed onto us without adequate warning, without support to guide us through the process, and without the knowledge of how we will be affected, we push back against the change due to our fear of the unknown.

2. Loss of control

This resistance comes because we prefer to be in control of our own destinies. After all, almost every personal development book in the world has told us we have this power! We like to create our own future and if things are out of our control we feel insecure and mistrustful of those involved, or mistrustful of the process of change and the eventual outcome.

3. Bad timing

If timing were everything, then we'd prefer change to happen according to our schedule. Many of us don't embrace change because we feel it isn't the right time (meaning we aren't prepared for the change). But is there *ever* a perfect time for change?

Personally, without advance warning and preparation, I've found it hard to cope with any type of change. And then, even with advance warning, navigating the process was hindered by the emotions that inevitably surfaced.

The risk of a crisis of confidence

Some of you might be thinking that this emotional stuff is not what you want to deal with right now. "Tell me which direction to take! Show me how to write a great cover letter and tweak my resume – I just want my next job!"

In our impatience to start earning another income, what we don't realise is that the shock of losing our last job, or difficult circumstances at our current one, can actually hinder us from finding our next position. After all, a job loss, especially an unexpected one, causes us to question everything. Whether our abilities were a poor match for the position or our role was made redundant by a restructure, we're left wondering:

Am I really cut out for this career?

Beyond the sense of injustice or anger a job loss might spark, underneath it all it's really a blow to our confidence in our abilities. Couple this with other life changes that might come up and we can get really shaken.

Brian Quirke, director of PHR Consulting, understands this better than most. After working with the State Bank of NSW for 29 years, in the mid-1990s Brian was made redundant after an acquisition by the Colonial Insurance Group. At the time he'd been Group HR Director and had also managed the metropolitan retail branch network of 3,000 staff.

He says, *"While I expected the retrenchment and in many ways looked forward to leaving the bank, it was still a very significant change in my life and one for which I was entirely unprepared. Suddenly I had no clear plan or identity, my networks outside banking were weak and I no real idea of what I wanted to do next.*

"I went at speed from being an 'important person' to an 'unemployed person'. I lost the things that I thought defined me – the status, the

car, the income – and, like many people, I was wandering in 'the mist' a bit."

And Brian isn't alone, with many of my clients sharing similar experiences. Here's what some of them told me:

"The hardest part of my redundancy was the loss of sense of self that I derived from my job, the inability to plan ahead, the realisation that after 30 years in only two companies it would be difficult to find a new role."

"I was anxious, concerned, sick in the stomach, couldn't sleep and was getting headaches. The hardest thing was getting other people to see my concerns and keeping my wits about me (trying not to let my self-confidence diminish)."

"I experienced negative effects of the stress of transition as I resorted to comfort eating and gained a lot of weight. This affected my confidence and I lost my focus and direction."

"Going through redundancy after 35 years in a stable government job and facing the incredible unknown for which I was ill prepared left me at a complete loss. The fact that I was unemployed at that dangerous age of 52, I felt like an 'old man' in the eyes of younger employees. I felt panic, I kept asking myself, "Why me?" I wondered what was wrong with me. I'd assumed I would work in the same organisation forever. I'd never considered that I'd have to find another job. The job was me. I'd had such a sheltered career, and when I wasn't there any more I felt [as if] an arm had been cut off."

This lack of confidence comes through when we start going for new positions, and if an employer has to choose between two people with the same qualifications and experience, they're going to choose the person who projects the most confidence and conviction that they can grow and thrive in the new position.

This is why, before we get to the tactical knowledge, you need to present yourself well on paper, online and in person; you need to build your confidence and resilience. Then you will know that you can safely navigate any change – even if it's unexpected.

How to survive an unexpected career change

... and position yourself for the next step in your career

So how can you maintain your confidence through unexpected changes, and courageously secure a new position?

I've been fortunate to coach many clients through their career transitions and personal challenges, and wanted to write a book to share my own experiences, and some of theirs, that would reach and make a difference in the lives of even more people.

After much thought, much research and lots of procrastination, I bit the bullet and put pen to paper (well, fingers to keyboard) to provide the practical steps that have worked for others and will guide you through the fog and towards clarity.

This book addresses the seven deadly mistakes of job hunters:

1. Lacking confidence and clarity
2. Not knowing what's most important
3. Having haphazard written and oral communication strategies
4. Presenting an image that lacks power and authenticity
5. Not understanding how to leverage all job search methods
6. Not being able to convey value in interviews
7. Not understanding the strategies for career success

Navigating Career Crossroads: How to Thrive When Changing Direction addresses all of these mistakes so you can make your transition smoothly.

This book covers my CAREERS methodology – seven steps to take control after a major career change that will lead you confidently to a new role suited to your core values, preferences, skills and knowledge.

The result of following the CAREERS program is that:

1. You will feel worthy and of value, confident in your capabilities and able to handle multiple changes in your life.
2. You will discover your passion, be clear on what you want and how to get it.
3. You will be well prepared to launch your marketing campaign, expand your network and create the career of your dreams.

Here's what we'll cover:

4. C: Confidently manage change

The first step involves building your confidence so you can thrive in any major change, whether it's a redundancy, working with a new boss, or even taking on new responsibilities. You'll learn techniques to manage the stress of major life changes, rebuild your self-confidence and develop personal resilience.

5. A: Assess what makes you tick

If you're looking for a new role, there's groundwork to be done before you go to market. You need to be clear about what you want, as well as what you can offer any potential employer, so that you're ready to sell yourself in person, on paper and online when the right opportunity emerges.

6. R: Resumes and your marketing communications

Here's where we get tactical. Using the knowledge gained in *Assess what makes you tick*, you'll discover how to write a compelling verbal pitch, prepare your resume and cover letter, and create a LinkedIn profile that has recruiters and employers seeking *you* out.

7. E: Express your professional image and personal brand

We all know that first impressions count, but have you really considered more than the visual impact you're making? In this section we'll go through the 5 essential aspects of your personal brand and how you can dress for success to present yourself as the perfect candidate for your ideal role.

8. E: Explore job search strategies that work

Many job seekers spend their days replying to online job ads, wondering why they aren't getting anywhere. In this chapter you'll learn about the most effective job-search strategies, and how to use them to get in front of the right people.

9. R: Relate your value and impress at interviews

Here you'll discover the secrets to interview success, including how to prepare and what to do before, during and after the interview.

10. S: Strategies for career success

When you receive the offer, it will be time to negotiate for what's most important to you. Then, when the contract is signed, you'll learn how to make a great impression in your new role!

As a bonus, throughout this book you will be given links to relevant useful resources you can download immediately for additional support, exploration and research.

So flip the pages to where your desire or need takes you.

For additional support, visit The Careers Academy where you'll find many free career management resources. I'd love you to join me in The Careers Academy for career transition support, and ongoing career management support to help you progress in your new role! Visit me here: www.thecareersacademy.online

CONFIDENTLY MANAGE CHANGE

"We cannot change anything until we accept it."

— Carl Jung

Do people think you're more confident than you really feel? Have you perfected your face for the world, your protective armour, so that you seem in control all, or most, of the time?

I think I've created a pretty good façade of self-confidence, and most of the time I do feel confident in myself. However, there were times when I felt self-doubt, unsure whether or not my choices or actions were the right ones for myself or for others and I questioned if I really knew what I was doing. Have you felt that too?

Way back when you and I were born, kicking and screaming into the world, we were very confident. We demanded air, we demanded to be fed, we demanded to be clothed, and we demanded to be cleaned because we deserved to be taken care of, nurtured, educated and loved.

For a time things went according to plan – we asked, and we received.

Then stuff happened. We either got what we needed or we didn't.

That influenced the way we now perceive the world. It's either a place filled with warmth and light all of the time; a place filled with some warmth and some light some of the time; a cold, dark place where we have to fight to survive; or we just drift and expect nothing much out of our existence.

So if you've lost your job, or are thinking about a career change, think of where you are on that scale. Do you believe there are opportunities for you in the job market and there are companies looking for exactly what you have to offer? Or do you see a difficult economy, where companies are downsizing, and you're worried you could be waiting months before you get a steady income again?

It's not easy to feel and act confident when we're experiencing change in our careers and lives. We lack certainty, we are unknowing, exploring and experimenting and this can be a confusing time. Change is stressful, and a job loss is one of the major stressors in our lives.

But what are the other stressors, and how may *they* be affecting your confidence when you go to market?

The impact of stress on your confidence

According to Holmes, TH & Rahe, RH (1967) in their study, *The Social Readjustment Scale*, various changes can have a significant impact on our stress levels.

Review the following life events and mark each of the events you have experienced in the last two years. Then add up your total score.

Life event	Average stress score*	Your score
Death of a spouse or partner	100	
Divorce	73	
Marital separation	65	
Death of close family member	63	
Personal injury or illness	53	
Marriage	50	
Job loss	47	
Marital reconciliation	45	
Retirement	45	
Change in health of family member	44	
Pregnancy	40	
Sexual difficulties	39	
New family member	39	
Business readjustment	39	
Change in finances	38	
Death of a close friend	37	
Change to different line of work	36	
Change in number of arguments with spouse/partner	35	
Mortgage or loan for a major purchase	31	
Foreclosure of mortgage or loan	30	

Life event	Average stress score*	Your score
Change in responsibilities at work	29	
Son or daughter leaving home	29	
Trouble with in-laws	29	
Outstanding personal achievement	28	
Spouse begins or stops work	26	
Beginning or finishing school	26	
Change in living conditions	25	
Revision of personal habits	24	
Trouble with boss	23	
Change in work hours or conditions	20	
Change in residence	20	
Change in schools	20	
Change in recreation	19	
Change in church activities	19	
Change in social activities	18	
Mortgage or loan for minor purchase	17	
Change in sleeping habits	16	
Change in number of family get-togethers	15	
Change in eating habits	15	
Vacation	13	
Christmas/holiday season	12	
Minor violations of the law	11	
TOTAL SCORE		

Please note that the individual stress scores in this survey are averages over many people, and the degree to which any particular event is stressful to you will depend on how you perceive it. Simply use these as a guide.

How did you score?

Under 150

If your total stress score is less than 150, you are less likely to be suffering the effects of cumulative stress.

150–300

If your total stress score is between 150 and 300, you may be suffering from chronic stress, depending on how you perceive and cope with the particular life events that occurred.

Over 300

If your total stress score is over 300, it is likely that you are experiencing some detrimental effects of cumulative stress.

What does this mean?

If you are suffering the effects of cumulative stress, you may be experiencing some of the following physical, mental and emotional symptoms that are typical of what people with high stress levels may experience.

Physical symptoms

- Sleeping more than normal
- Not sleeping enough or difficulty sleeping
- Weight gain or weight loss
- Constantly feeling tired
- Stomach trouble or pain
- Sexual problems
- Overuse of alcohol or drugs
- Chronic physical problems (such as indigestion, diarrhoea, constipation)
- Neck aches or back aches
- Overeating or loss of appetite
- Headaches
- Other unusual physical symptoms

Mental symptoms

- Feeling under constant pressure
- Feeling lonely or isolated
- Catastrophic thinking or over-personalising situations
- Feeling vulnerable to the criticism of others
- Feeling misunderstood
- Denial of problems
- Difficulty asking for help
- Difficulty making decisions
- Feeling left out or rejected
- Feeling anger
- Worrying more than normal
- Feeling obsessed with unobtainable goals
- Frequently feeling sad
- Unable to enjoy what used to be pleasurable
- Feeling trapped
- Feeling insecure or undeserving of affection
- Exaggerating your own importance to yourself and others
- Other unusual mental symptoms

Behavioural symptoms

- Deteriorating personal relationships
- Withdrawing from friends, family and colleagues
- Frequent arguments with your partner
- Problems with authority figures
- Avoiding responsibilities you used to welcome
- Developing a pattern of lateness
- Neglecting your appearance
- Forgetting important commitments
- Going to extremes (spending, gambling, compulsive habits)
- Working too hard or too long
- Perfectionism taken to the extreme
- Other behavioural symptoms

IMPORTANT: Visit your GP for professional advice if the symptoms you've identified are severe or have been ongoing, as there may be underlying physical factors causing or aggravating the symptoms.

How will this affect your career?

Whether you're looking for a new job, trying to get a promotion, or simply want to perform your current role to the best of your ability, it's essential you realise the impact that stress and its symptoms can have on your career.

As an example, if you're having difficulty sleeping, you're not able to perform as well at work, with sleep deprivation resulting in confusion and poor memory, irritability, and headaches.

From a mental perspective, if you feel lonely or isolated, you're going to find it more difficult to relate to others, and you'll experience less enjoyment at work. If you have difficulty making decisions or asking for help, you aren't going to be able to do your work as efficiently.

If you're experiencing some behavioural symptoms, you're going to find it more difficult to relate to others in the workplace, be they managers, colleagues or prospective employers.

The key to confidence – understanding change

So how can we build up our self-confidence during periods of change, so we can command the careers we want?

Managing stress

I've experienced a number of the symptoms of stress at various stages in my life – they occurred when my father passed away when I was 11, and when my mother passed away more recently, when I was anxious about moving to a new country or new home (I've managed five country moves and numerous house moves), when I was about to get married (both times!) and most certainly when I was going through my divorce, which resulted in a country move and having to settle my teenage daughters into a new school in a completely unfamiliar environment and system. Multiple stressors definitely contributed to my anxiety and lowered my self-confidence.

So what did I do? I took these five steps to gain control of my life, and always keep this as my action plan to keep my cool during stressful circumstances. Beyond dealing with change, you'll find these techniques helpful during other stressful situations, including job interviews.

1. Talk

Find someone you trust and respect and talk to them about your concerns. Letting it out frequently relieves stress and the old saying, "a problem shared is a problem halved" always rings true.

It also helps to know that you're not alone. Brian Quirke, Director of PHR Consulting, whom we met in the introduction, discovered this when he started sharing his experience of workplace bullying with his colleagues:

"When I discovered that [my manager] was doing the same thing to all of the other male State Managers, I knew it wasn't just me. This was a very big step forward and was when I decided to push back, take back my control and work hard at finding a new challenge."

When I asked Brian if there was anything he would have done differently, he admits that he now recognises the importance of getting support from others. *"In hindsight I should have sought the counsel of someone far wiser than I was. I think we're often too reluctant (males in particular) to admit that we're not coping well –*

I should have found a wise owl to coach me through it. The outcome may have been the same but the angst far less."

Likewise, these comments from some of my private coaching clients confirm that talking to others is invaluable.

"I'd talk the issues through with my husband. (He is always great with work issues.) His mantra is, 'It is what it is ... what are you going to do about it?' I'd talk to my parents (wise and experienced minds always have a different view), and I got advice from my coach who was great at providing a clear and effective direction."

"Venting about issues over a red wine or a coffee is my best medicine. I also found talking candidly with management and HR about how to make decisions when facing tough times was helpful."

"I saw a GP to help me handle my stress. When I found I had trouble sleeping and it wasn't getting any better, I also saw a therapist who gave me space to focus on organising my thoughts. The therapist showed me that I had to acknowledge what I was feeling. Having that outlet was a big step. Initially I felt 'How Eastern suburbs am I to be seeing a therapist?' but it wasn't fair to rely too much on family and friends. When the stress became all-consuming, I needed professional help."

When reaching out to family or friends, remember to talk to them about *their* concerns or problems too. This helps put your experiences into perspective.

One of the things that really helped me when I was going through my divorce and moved from Singapore to Sydney was to continue my work as a career coach. Working with those who had gone through a redundancy and were feeling anxious about their futures gave me a positive focus – helping them through their situation. Helping them helped me get through my personal challenges. The knowledge that I was not the only one going through some tough stuff was a huge reality check for me.

2. Think

Your thoughts have a huge impact on how you feel, so focus on creating thoughts that keep you calm and centred, rather than ones that ramp up your anxiety.

Start by **stopping irrational thinking** and vague, general self-talk and assumptions such as, "I'll never get over this," "No one cares about me," "I'll never get another job," "I'm over the hill." Self-pity keeps you stuck in the negative situation.

Instead, **choose positive self-talk**. First of all, listen to the voice in your head. What's it telling you when you are feeling stressed? Is it judging you? Is it criticising you? Has the voice crawled out of your head, turned into a self-limiting belief and now sitting on your shoulder, whispering negativity into your ear? Positive self-talk needs to drown out the negative voices in your head and knock the nasty self-limiting belief off your shoulder.

You can use your new, positive thoughts as **positive affirmations**. "I will get over this," "Someone does care about me," "I'll get another job, I'll make it happen," "I'm a vibrant and valuable professional," "I deserve to be loved," "This, too, shall pass."

Positive affirmations are a great way to start your day, so give them a go for seven days and see how you feel! Even if you are sceptical, what have you got to lose? There is so much to gain by telling yourself: "I am willing to give affirmations a try each morning for seven days. I am willing to be surprised and inspired by the power of my own words."

If you're struggling to think of some affirmations, here are seven morning affirmations to repeat three times every morning when you wake up. It will take you about 60 seconds to create a great day.

7 Morning Affirmations

1. I feel healthy and strong today.
2. I have all I need to make today a great day.
3. I have it within me to solve any challenges that occur today.
4. I am able to make smart decisions for myself today.
5. I am happy and content with my life.
6. I am patient and calm and looking forward to today.
7. I am grateful for another day to make a positive contribution.

3. Sweat

According to the Australian Psychological Society, regular exercise will help to reduce anxiety by providing an outlet to let off stress that has built up in your body. Exercise also strengthens the body and enables you to better withstand stress.

One of my clients, the Financial Controller of a global IT organisation, describes how exercise helped him manage his stress when he went through his redundancy, "Exercise worked best for me. Even a 5km run changed my mood to a positive one. Also, having something to look forward to, like an organised 12km Bay to Bay run or a weekend motorcycle trip, helped a lot."

As the Australian Government Department of Health says, "Being physically active and limiting your sedentary behaviour every day is essential for health and wellbeing. These guidelines are for all adults aged 18–64 years, irrespective of cultural background, gender or ability."

Their physical activity guidelines include:
- Be active on most, preferably all, days every week.
- Accumulate 2½ to 5 hours of moderate intensity physical

activity, or 1¼ to 2½ hours of vigorous intensity physical activity, or an equivalent combination each week.
- Do muscle-strengthening activities on at least two days each week.
- If you currently do no physical activity, start by doing some and gradually build up to the recommended amount.

What works for me:

- Jogging, walking or dancing three to five times a week for 20–30 minutes. When the weather is bad, I go up and down the stairwell in our apartment block for 20–30 minutes. An indoor stairwell can get rather boring so I download a podcast and listen to that on my iPhone while I'm climbing up and down the stairs. (What would I do without my iPhone?)
- I've found small daily goals and consistency work better than perfect workouts. It's better to walk every day for 15–20 minutes than to wait until the weekend for a three-hour fitness marathon. For something to become a habit, it needs to be done regularly, and I've found that once exercise becomes a habit, I feel better in other areas of my life too.
- Find forms of exercise that are fun or enjoyable. Choose what works for YOU, otherwise you won't keep it up. Consider group exercise classes or other group activities such as running, cycling or dancing. You can find groups that appeal to you by having a look on www.meetup.com. Most of these groups are free and, if you can't find one you like in your area, you can create one yourself!
- Recruit an "exercise buddy." It's often easier to stick to your exercise routine when you have to stay committed to a friend, partner or colleague. That way you have someone to talk to and you can help your buddy get fitter and manage his or her stress levels too.

Remember to be patient when you start a new exercise program. Most sedentary people require about four to eight weeks to feel sufficiently in shape so that exercise feels easier. And, if you have any health issues or haven't exercised for a long time, check with your GP before embarking on any form of exercise programme.

Beyond the Department of Health suggestions, just take a brisk walk instead of driving or taking a bus, walk to where you want to go, or park a little further away and walk to your destination. It's amazing what a little bit of extra physical activity can do to manage your stress levels.

4. Organise

One of the things that stresses a lot of us is feeling like we can't manage everything on our plate. Taking a few small actions can help you feel far more organised, and far less stressed.

First, write things down! When you feel stressed it's so easy to lose track of things – little details such as appointments, shopping items, birthdays and special occasions. Get a planner system, use your Outlook Calendar or iCal and refer to it each evening so you can prepare yourself for the next day.

Next, plan enjoyable activities for yourself and others. Just planning a holiday makes you feel better – there's nothing wrong with a dream that makes you feel good inside.

Finally, plan your activities in advance so that they don't become urgent and even more stressful. A great time management tool is the Time Management Matrix from *First Things First* by Stephen R. Covey. Once you learn the basics of organising your activities according to the principles of this tool, you'll be able to eliminate a number of your time-wasting activities and unproductive behaviours and ensure your daily stressors are minimised.

Covey's matrix groups activities into four quadrants:
- Important and Urgent
- Important and Non-Urgent
- Non-Important and Urgent
- Non-Important and Non-Urgent

	URGENT	NON-URGENT
IMPORTANT	Quadrant 1 Necessity – manage this Crises Deadline-driven activities Medical emergencies Other real emergencies Major problems Last-minute stuff	Quadrant 2 Personal leadership – focus on this Preparation Planning Identifying values Relationship building Self-empowerment Time to rest and relax
NON-IMPORTANT	Quadrant 3 Deceptive urgency – be cautious Other people's requirements Frequent interruptions Many emails and calls Urgency that appears important	Quadrant 4 Wasteful – try to avoid Procrastination/escapism Mindless television 'Busywork' Some emails Some calls

Adapted from Steven Covey's *First Things First* – Covey Leadership Center Inc. ©2003

Now evaluate your current situation – make a list of your daily activities and identify the quadrant where each belongs. In which quadrant do you spend most of your time each day?

To create a positive change in your daily schedule, aim to spend the most time in Quadrant 2. How? You need to start planning your time in advance – making time for activities in Quadrant 2, filling your schedule so you aren't wasting time in Quadrant 4 and only allocating limited time to activities in Quadrant 3 (e.g., only checking emails twice a day).

By devoting a good deal of time to Quadrant 2, you will naturally eliminate many of the crises that tend to happen in Quadrant 1 and it will give you solid direction that, in turn, will help eliminate spending excess time in the other Quadrants.

Preparation and planning is the key to successful time management and stress reduction.

5. Act

Taking action gets you moving forward. You just have to do it! So how can you get yourself moving?

The first thing you need to do is to **stop striving for perfection**. If you have unrealistic expectations for yourself you will put yourself under enormous pressure, which leads to more stress and makes it unlikely that you'll act. Focus more on the enjoyment of what you are doing in any given moment rather than achieving the perfect result every time.

Next, **analyse situations and people that cause you stress**. How can you avoid those situations and minimise contact with those people who are confrontational or negative? How can you minimise their impact on you if you can't avoid specific stressful situations or people?

If you know that there will potentially be stressful situations during the day, create a personal action plan for yourself. Know what you will do to remain calm rather than reacting when not thinking clearly. Decide what works best for you for various situations.

Will you take a deep breath before saying anything?

Will you take a minute to observe the situation and assess the best plan of action?

Will you ask for more time before responding? Will you smile and ask for more information first?

Will you simply say that you need time to consider all options?

I've found what works for me, before reacting to any challenging interaction, is to imagine I'm a fly on the wall. I look at the situation from my own viewpoint and also put myself in the shoes of the others around me. It helps me to consider what would be motivating the others to act or react in that particular way. I call this 'perceptual positioning', which is a technique I learned when I qualified as a Neuro Linguistic Programming (NLP) practitioner. This strategy helps me stay objective and act with more understanding.

Next, choose to act happy. You can fool your body systems into reducing stress reactions if you act happy, particularly by using your body language. Even when you don't feel cheerful, smile, stand upright and lift your head – you'll be surprised by the difference it makes.

As spoken by Thich Nhat Hanh, who was nominated for the Nobel Peace Prize in 1967 by Martin Luther King, Jr., *"Sometimes your joy is the source of your smile, but sometimes your smile can be the source of your joy."*

Choose to soothe yourself. Use relaxation techniques to relax your mind and body. Massage, meditation and yoga are all techniques that help to physically relax your body and quieten your mind during times of stress.

Here's a simple technique that works for me, one that I've shared with many friends, family members and also my career transition clients.

The Spirit of Confidence – Visualisation and Meditation

Find a comfortable, quiet spot where you won't be disturbed for 15–20 minutes. Sit and settle in, either crossed-legged on the floor or on a chair. Close your eyes and take a moment to become aware of yourself.

Take a deep breath in for five counts and exhale slowly for five counts. Keep breathing to a count of five in and five out, and become aware of how you feel. Are you sitting comfortably? Make any adjustments so that you are comfortable. Roll your shoulders up, back and down slowly to relax, and repeat.

Then tilt your head to the left so your left ear reaches towards your left shoulder. Slowly roll your chin towards your chest and your right ear towards your right shoulder and then your chin towards your chest again. Bring your head up slowly and breathe – five in, five out.

As you relax, imagine that you are standing at the edge of a giant, friendly forest. It's inviting you in and you enter this wonderful forest filled with fresh, green smells and the sound of peace and quiet.

As you wander deeper into the forest you notice that the sun leaves speckles of light on your shoulders as it peeps through the leaves and branches above you. You feel good.

All around you are beautiful trees and plants; the occasional butterfly darts around you and flutters away. You notice that the leaves crunch beneath you and in the dappled light you can see that they are a lovely mix of autumnal colours – deep browns and ochres – just beautiful. You take a deep breath and the smell is intoxicatingly fresh. You smile and feel at peace.

You wander deeper into the forest and with every step you relax more and more. You feel happy. You feel light. You feel safe. You are smiling.

You take another deep breath and exhale slowly. As you do, you hear the sound of water in the distance. It draws you in. You follow the path towards the sound of the water, the leaves crunching under your feet, the sun dancing through the leaves of the trees. As you walk you notice that the water sounds as if it's a running stream. Gentle and inviting.

You get closer and see through a clearing in the trees that it is a stream. The sun on the water looks like diamonds –

millions of diamonds sparkling beautifully as the water dances across the pebbles.

You take off your shoes at the edge of the stream and take a cooling step into the liquid diamonds. There is a large flat rock nearby and you climb on to it to lie down. You lie back and shield your eyes from the sunlight. It's so beautiful here.

You take a deep breath and slowly exhale. As you do so you notice that there is something dancing in the sky, far away. You watch it curiously as it dances in the sky, moving with the breeze. It gets closer to you and closer to you and you realise it's a balloon in your favourite colour. Stunning against the sky. You want to touch it. The breeze pushes it closer to you and closer to you and you reach out. You can almost touch it. Then whoosh! It's blown upwards and away. But that's okay. You're happy to let it go and you watch as it floats higher and higher and higher until it disappears. You are relaxed. You are happy to be right here, right now. And it's quiet.

As your mind remains quiet, bring into the back of your mind a word, any word, that will be your mantra. It can be a word with no meaning, or it can be 'calm', 'peace', or 'om'. I use 'aying', a word with no meaning that relaxes me.

In the back of your mind, bring the mantra gently into being. Repeat it over and over again slowly, focusing on the word. Just the word. Nothing else. Over and over and over again. Nothing matters except for the word. Focus on the word.

While you cannot clear your head of thoughts, you can replace those thoughts with your word, your mantra. As you focus on your mantra, your mind will play tricks on you and start to think thoughts. Just let them go and return to your mantra. Each time you catch yourself thinking thoughts, return to your mantra.

> Keep repeating your mantra and breathe. Repeat your mantra and breathe ...
>
> After 10–20 minutes (set a gentle-sounding alarm if required), slowly bring yourself out of your meditation by taking a deeper breath and becoming aware of your body again. Become aware of your toes, your legs, your buttocks, your torso, your arms, your hands and your fingers. Become aware of your shoulders and face. Roll your shoulders up, back and down. And again. Take a deep breath and, when you are ready, slowly open your eyes and smile.

How do you feel now?

You will find the audio recording of this guided visualisation and meditation on YOUR CAREER Podcast (look for it on iTunes, Spotify or Stitcher Radio). You can download it on to your iPhone or media player, and, each day, gift yourself a few minutes to relax and refocus your mind. Here's the direct link to my podcast - the meditation is episode 94 – www.janejacksoncoach.com/podcast

Remember to **keep it simple**. Sometimes all it takes is to do something different to give you a more relaxed perspective on things. Here are three things you can do and each will only take 30–60 seconds:

1. Stand up and stretch.
2. Breathe deeply – count five in and five out.
3. Laugh – just belly laugh. (Yes, for no reason – just laugh!)

Changing your relationship with change

These stress-reduction techniques will certainly help you to manage your stress levels, however it's best to recognise that our relationship with change is what's causing the stress, and then learn to deal with that relationship.

Change is a constant feature in our lives and careers, and learning to accept it rather than fight it is a key step to creating full and happy lives.

So, if it is a career transition or another major life transition you are going through that is creating the stress, keep the following in mind to sail a little more smoothly through each stage:

Stage 1: Endings

- Give it time.
- Maintain open communication with significant people in your life about your feelings.
- List gains and losses from the change.
- Acknowledge the value from the past.
- List what is positive about the change.
- Focus forward – don't look in the rear-view mirror.

Stage 2: The Neutral Zone

- Give it time.
- Set up a structure to your day.
- Talk to others to create a support group.
- Take care of your health – exercise, nutrition.
- Do the small stuff really well.
- Volunteer to help others.
- Learn something new.
- Celebrate little wins.
- Keep a journal of what's happening every day.
- Say your morning affirmations every day.
- Research and explore possibilities.

Stage 3: The New Beginning

- Give it time.
- Celebrate your progress.

- Enjoy what feels new.
- Visualise success.
- Stay connected to your support group.
- Maintain clear and open communication at all times.
- Seek feedback and stay in touch with old friends.
- Take action.
- Continue your positive self-talk and create new daily affirmations.

Regardless of the stage you're going through, remember:

- Change is an external event leading to internal transition.
- There is no beginning without an ending.
- Before any new beginning there is always a period of exploration.
- Transition is rarely smooth – there are no shortcuts.
- There is a reason for the process.
- There can be multiple changes and transitions happening at any given time.

Managing your stress and being aware of your transition process will give you the strength to remain confident in the face of change, and embark on your search for a new career.

If stress ever gets too much for you please see your doctor for professional advice. A good website where you will find information on how to manage anxiety and stress is: www.beyondblue.org.au.

ASSESS WHAT MAKES YOU TICK

"Alice: Would you tell me, please, which way I ought to go from here?

The Cheshire Cat: That depends a good deal on where you want to get to.

Alice: I don't much care where.

The Cheshire Cat: Then it doesn't much matter which way you go.

Alice: … So long as I get somewhere.

The Cheshire Cat: Oh, you're sure to do that, if only you walk long enough."

— Lewis Carroll, Alice in Wonderland

Are you feeling stuck when it comes to what to do next in your career because your role has recently been made redundant, or are you trapped in a job you hate? Or maybe you're in a job that's okay, but you feel there is so much more you could do to realise your potential.

Whether you want to re-enter the workforce after a break, you want to rebuild your career after a redundancy, or you just want a change because you are sick and tired of your job and need something more fulfilling, then this chapter is for you!

This chapter will get you clear on your values, motivators, strengths, achievements, and the dream job you want to achieve. After all, as the Cheshire Cat tells us, if we don't know where we want to go, then any road will get us there.

But can't I just skip to the resume and interview chapters? Well, you could … but I wouldn't recommend it because in the next few pages you'll find step-by-step exercises that will help you attract the job you'll love.

Why is this important? If you're stuck in a job you don't like, or your previous job was one that you weren't that satisfied with, you will be fully aware of what it's like to spend over eight hours a day, every day, doing something that just isn't 'you'.

If you keep doing something you don't enjoy, it affects the way you feel about yourself, your relationships, and every other aspect of your life. I know this so well because I once took on a job that just wasn't right for me – it was a role that required me to work in a way that was outside of my natural behaviour and at the time I thought I would be able to excel. Now, I'm very consultative in my approach and enjoy relationship-building and coaching to bring out the best in others, yet the new role I took on was all about meeting daily sales targets and had a transactional, deadline-driven sales focus. None of these fit with my natural behaviours. I found that the values and behaviour of senior management also did not gel with my personal and career values; every day was a battle.

I was so stressed going in to work in the mornings that my husband noticed a radical change in my demeanour. I'm a naturally easy-going and happy person with a very positive outlook. Well, I wasn't very positive during my time in that job! After work I would be so exhausted that I wouldn't want to do anything except flop in front of the telly and I didn't want to talk.

I found that I was more emotional than normal and during the months before I finally resigned I'd feel tearful at the smallest setbacks. This was so out of character that I thought there was something wrong with me. Upon careful analysis I found there was nothing wrong with me – I was just in the wrong job!

When I bit the bullet and resigned it was as if a cloud had lifted. I went back to doing what I loved more than anything in the world – coaching. I love to listen to others' concerns, working to help them through their challenges; not trying to sell anything, just making a difference in people's lives every day. I had a spring in my step again and every day I would look forward to meeting new clients, doing what I felt was really worthwhile. It's what I'm doing now and, for as long as I am able, will continue to do!

What about you? What's important to you and what do you really want? I've seen so many people at a loss as they try to please their loved ones, their parents, their teachers, their managers and take on roles that were not right for them. This has resulted in dissatisfaction, frustration and a loss of identity.

It's now time to make the right decisions for *you*! When you have clarity about what is important to you, you will be able to come across as the authentic professional you truly are during the interview process. You will also be able to turn down offers that are not right for you.

Everyone can get a job, any job. You could get a job tomorrow if you wanted to, but it mightn't be the right job for you – it might not pay the salary that you are worth, it might not be as motivating as you'd like it to be.

Getting *a* job is not the issue; it's getting the *right* job for you. So where do you start?

There are some basic questions you need to ask yourself to identify the ideal career for you:

1. Where am I in my life right now? (Life Inventory.)
2. What's important to me in my career? (Values.)
3. What makes me feel satisfied at work and what demotivates me? (Motivators and demotivators.)
4. What can I do and what am I good at? (Skills and knowledge.)
5. What have I done in my previous roles that actually made a difference to the company/department/team? (Your achievements.)
6. What is my dream job? (Work preferences, location, job function, industry, salary level, flexibility at work, company culture and so on.)

Let's get started!

Give yourself three to four hours over the next few days to complete the following six exercises (or all on one day if you have the time) to seriously think about your responses. This is preparing for the rest of your life so you owe it to yourself to take care of what is important to you. I'd like you to focus on what is important to YOU, not anyone else, while completing these exercises.

1. Your life inventory

We're all so busy in our lives that often we forget exactly where we are right now. Where are you in your life today? Where are you when it comes to your relationships, your career, your finances, your environment, your health and your emotional balance?

If any of these aspects of your life are out of balance, you will find that you feel drained of energy. When you start to take control of your life and tackle each niggly little thing that you are tolerating, you will find that you have more energy, you feel mentally lighter and emotionally stronger too so you can focus your energies on your career transition.

This Life Inventory will help you to get back on track. However, it's not a quick fix. Once you've completed your Life Inventory the aim is that, within the next six months, you will become aware of what is important to you and make a positive difference in your life.

Instructions:

7. Read each statement and tick the box *only if it is true for you*. This is your Life Inventory so if you need to change a statement to fit your situation better, you can do so.
8. Add up the number of ticks to get your total score for each section.
9. Write your total for all areas in the 'start date' box in the Life Inventory chart on page 45. Then, commit to checking in again in 90 days (your interim date) and 180 days (your end date).
10. Fill in the Life Inventory Chart working from the bottom up. Colour in one box for each tick you have given yourself in each section. You have a maximum of 20 boxes to colour in for each section.
11. Whenever you have taken care of another aspect of your life and are able to tick off another statement, colour in another box in the corresponding section.
12. The aim is to colour in as many boxes as you can as this will show you are taking action on what is important to you regarding your finances, relationships, home, health and career.

Finances

☐ My income is stable and predictable.

☐ I currently save at least 10% of my income. I pay my bills on time, almost always.

☐ I know what I need to become financially independent, and I have a plan.

☐ I have agreements with anyone to whom I owe money and my payments are up to date.

☐ I have six months' living expenses in a savings account.

☐ I live on a weekly budget that allows me to save and live comfortably.

☐ My tax returns have been filed, and my taxes have been paid. I currently live comfortably within my means.

☐ I have excellent medical insurance.

☐ My assets (car, home, possessions, treasures) are insured. I have a financial plan for the next year.

☐ I have no legal issues that require attention. My will is up to date.

☐ My investments don't keep me awake at night. I know what I am worth financially.

☐ I have good working relationships with people who can help my career.

☐ I'm rarely sick or need to take time off.

☐ I am saving enough money each month to reach financial independence.

☐ My income keeps up with or exceeds inflation.

Total _____

Relationships

- People can trust and count on me.
- In the last two months, I have told my parents that I loved them.
- I get along well with my sibling(s).
- If miscommunications or misunderstandings occur I quickly clear them up.
- I have a circle of friends and/or family who love me for who I am, more than just what I do for them.
- I don't judge others.
- I am open and don't take personally the things that people say to me.
- I have a best friend or soul mate.
- There is no one I would feel uncomfortable meeting (whether at a party or in the street).
- I have let go of the relationships that drag me down. (I have ended, walked away from, handled, or am no longer attached to negative relationships.)
- I have tried to communicate with everyone I may have hurt in any way, even if it wasn't totally my fault.
- I don't gossip.
- I let people know how they can satisfy me and what I need from them.
- I am always truthful.
- I receive enough love from people around me to feel good.
- I have forgiven those people who have hurt me, whether it was deliberate or not.
- I live life on my own terms, not on the terms of others. There is nothing unresolved with my past loves or partners. I know my wants and needs and get them taken care of.
- I spend time with people who make me feel good and don't try to change me.

Total _____

Home front

- My home is neat and clean (vacuumed, furniture in good repair, windows clean).
- My car is in excellent condition (doesn't need cleaning, repairs). All my appliances and equipment work well.
- All my clothes are all clean and pressed and make me look great.
- My plants and animals are healthy (loved and well-tended).
- My bed and bedroom let me have the best sleep possible (great bed, ventilation).
- I live in a place that I love.
- I surround myself with beautiful things. I live in the geographic area I choose.
- There is plenty of healthy light around me.
- I have adequate time, space, and freedom in my life.
- I am not harmed by my environment (power stations, unhealthy environment).
- I am not tolerating anything about my environment at home. I recycle and take care of the environment.
- I enjoy surrounding myself with music. I make my bed daily.
- I'm not clumsy and don't bump into things. People feel comfortable in my home.
- I drink purified water.
- I have de-cluttered my house and don't hoard what I don't need.

Total _____

Health

- I've had a full physical exam in the past three years and have been tested for AIDS and STD.
- My cholesterol count and blood pressure is normal.
- I have had a complete eye exam within the past two years (glaucoma check, vision test) and use sunglasses.
- I've seen a dentist in the last six months and my teeth and gums are healthy.
- My hearing is good.
- I am aware of the physical or emotional issues I have, and I am now fully taking care of all of them.
- I walk or exercise at least three times per week for 20 minutes.
- I regularly enjoy evenings, weekends, and holidays to relax and take at least two weeks' holiday every year.
- I rarely drink alcohol (fewer than three drinks per week). I have no bad habits that I'm ashamed of.
- I don't smoke.
- I do not use illegal drugs or misuse prescribed medications.
- I rarely have sugar with anything and don't crave sugary treats. I watch fewer than five hours of TV per week.
- My weight is within my ideal range.
- My nails, hair and skin are healthy and look good. I don't rush to get things done.
- I have interests I enjoy outside of my work.
- I have something to look forward to every day. I don't feel I am suffering in any way.

Total _____

Career

My work environment is productive and inspiring (good resources, not too much stress).

I am on a career track that is, or will soon be, financially and personally rewarding.

I spend time getting to know others across other areas in my company.

I take the time to learn new skills through training or offering to take on new projects.

I am earning what is fair compared to the time and effort I put into my work.

There are no loose ends I have to take care of at work.

I get along well with my manager, colleagues and clients. I put people first and results second.

I'm up to date with all my emails and calls. I don't complain; I state what I require.

My files, papers and receipts are neatly filed away or taken care of.

I'm not tolerating anything about my work. I am on time for meetings and never late.

I have a mentor who can guide me in my career.

I know where I'd like my career to take me in the next three to five years.

I understand what my career options are within my current workplace.

I look forward to going to work most days.

I am technically and functionally capable of performing well in my role.

I have as much autonomy as I need in my current role. I feel passionate about what I do and I do it well.

Total _____

Life Inventory Chart

Start date:	Interim date:	End date:
/100	/100	/100

	Finances	Relationships	Home front	Health	Career
20					
19					
18					
17					
16					
15					
14					
13					
12					
11					
10					
9					
8					
7					
6					
5					
4					
3					
2					
1					

Colour in each box in each column from the bottom up.

Keep adding to this chart as you tick off more items in the 5 Life Inventory sections.

2. Be clear on your values

Our values represent our deepest beliefs and guide us through our everyday life. Our values shape our opinions and our dreams. Our values are deeply embedded in our minds and spirits. If we know which values are the most important to us, we can find a way to increase our life and career satisfaction. And if we don't know which ones are important to us, we'll suffer a lot of physical, mental and emotional stress.

The following list includes examples of values from a career and a personal standpoint. As your career greatly affects your personal life, it is important for us to assess both.

Directions:

Look at the values listed and tick one of the four columns for each value – Extremely Important, Important, Perhaps, Never. Choose the column that best describes how consistently important each value has been to you.

Your priority values will be indicated by checks in the "Extremely Important" column.

Please do not exceed 10 checks in the "Extremely Important" column.

Values	EI	I	P	N
1. Personal growth: Develop my potential and use my talents				
2. Achievement: Have a sense of accomplishment and mastery				
3. Knowledge: Develop and use specific knowledge and expertise				
4. Status: Hold a position of fulfilment, importance in the organisation				
5. Competition: Engage in activities in which people must compete against each other				
6. Change and variety: Have job responsibilities with varied tasks				
7. Service to society: Contribute to a better society				
8. Physical activity: Do work requiring strength, agility, or physical exertion				
9. Independence: Control my own work/schedule				
10. Leadership: Influence others to achieve results				
11. Creative expression: Express my creativity and imagination in my work				
12. Challenge: Find work that mentally stimulates me				
13. Money: Reap significant financial rewards				
14. Security: Perform my work without worry about possible unemployment				
15. Management: Achieve work goals as a result of others' efforts				
16. Work with others: Belong to a satisfying work group or team				
17. **Power:** Have control over resources at work				
18. **Integrity:** Work ethically and honestly				

Values	EI	I	P	N
19. **Balance:** Achieve the right proportion between my personal life and professional responsibilities				
20. **Friendship:** Develop social/personal friendships with work colleagues				
21. **Career advancement:** Be promotable within the organisation				
22. **Detail work:** Deal with tasks that must meet specifications requiring careful, accurate attention to detail				
23. **Fast pace:** Work under time-pressured circumstances with demanding expectations				
24. **Helping others:** Involve myself in helping society and others				
25. **Location:** Live in a convenient geographic location in a suitable community				
26. **Recognition:** Receive credit for work well done				
27. **Excitement:** Enjoy frequent novelty and drama				
28. **Moral fulfilment:** Find work that contributes to moral ideas				
29. **Aesthetics:** Appreciate the beauty of things and ideas				
30. **Health:** Be physically and mentally fit				
31. **Positive atmosphere:** Work in a supportive, pleasing, harmonious setting				
32. **Efficient organisation:** Be in a time-efficient environment with little bureaucracy				
33. **Family happiness:** Maintain good balance between work and family life				

EI = Extremely Important, I = Important, P = Perhaps, N = Never

My top values

Now rank your values in order of importance to you. For example, if you had to choose between family and time freedom, which would it be? A forced ranking of values helps you to clarify your priorities. Such a process helps you to identify your most important values and when you take action to satisfy those values, you'll achieve greater personal fulfilment as a result.

Start by writing your 10 'Extremely Important' values below, then rank your top 5 values in the column on the right from 1 (the most important, non-negotiable driving value in your life) to 5.

My priority values	Rank

These top five values are those that make you happy, and the ones that relate to your career are the ones that should *not* be compromised in your next role if you want to be fulfilled and satisfied in your career.

3. Motivators/demotivators

Our workplace and environment can have a great impact on our motivation – when our key motivators are hit, we bounce out of bed in the morning excited to get to work and solve a problem or make a difference. When we are demotivated, we keep hitting the snooze button and groan when we can't put off waking up any longer.

So, write down what is or was satisfying and dissatisfying about your current, or most recent, company, position and manager to figure out what your motivators and demotivators are. Then do the same thing for the role before that.

Write down specifically what was great, what not so great – both big issues and little irritations – and include the reasons why. Take time to think about why you feel this way, as it is often in the "why" that we can gain clarity about what's most important for you to stay motivated in any role.

Motivators	What did you like?	Why?
Company		
Position		
Manager		

Demotivators	What did you dislike?	Why?
Company		
Position		
Manager		

4. Skills and knowledge identification

Your skills and knowledge will have a big impact on your career – not only concerning how attractive you are to potential employers, but also when it comes to how attractive potential positions are to you.

In the following tables, simply tick where you are highly skilled and where you have experience.

Skills and knowledge	Highly skilled	Experienced
General management & administration:		
Communication		
Contract negotiations		
Directing others		
Follow-up/control		
Licensing		
Organisational planning		
Pricing		

Skills and knowledge	Highly skilled	Experienced
Problem solving		
Project management		
Providing feedback		
Purchasing		
Regulatory reporting		
Scheduling		
Strategic analysis		
Strategic planning		
Team building		
Sales/marketing/customer service:		
Advertising		
Buying		
Competitive analysis		
Customer service		
Market analysis		
Fund raising		
Marketing		
New business development		
Pricing strategy		
Promotional writing		
Retailing		
Sales development		
Selling/influencing		
Finance & accounting:		
Accounting		
Audit		
Capital budgeting		
Cash management		

Skills and knowledge	Highly skilled	Experienced
Credit		
Debt negotiations		
Financial data processing		
Foreign exchange		
Cost accounting		
General tax planning		
Internal controls		
Inventory control analysis		
Management reporting		
Planning and analysis		
Pricing/forecast modelling		
Risk management		
Strategic financial planning		
Treasury		
Research & engineering:		
Diagnostics		
Field-applied research		
Licensing/patent strategy		
New product development		
Plant design & construction		
Process development		
Process engineering		
Research & development		
Technology commercialisation		
Human resources:		
Administration		
Benefits		
Career counselling		

Skills and knowledge	Highly skilled	Experienced
Career development		
Community relations		
Industrial relations		
Employee relations		
Executive recruiting		
Labour relations		
Organisation development		
Performance evaluation		
Planning		
Policy & procedures		
Safety and health		
Staff planning & management		
Team building		
Training & development		
Union negotiations		
Wage & salary		
Operations:		
Administration		
Budget planning		
Construction		
Customer service		
Distribution		
Engineering		
Expense control		
Inventory & production		
Management		
Materials management		
Process engineering		

Skills and knowledge	Highly skilled	Experienced
Procurement		
Production		
Project direction		
Quality assurance		
Systems development		
Warehousing		
Information systems:		
Business systems planning		
Communication carriers		
Data centre operation		
Database technology		
Diagnostics		
Distributive systems		
Hardware/software technology		
Information management		
Office automation		
Performance monitoring		
System design/programming		
Systems development		
Telecommunication networks		

5. Your dream role

I've been a career coach for over 14 years and over those years I've found that career success means something different to each and every one of my clients. What does career success mean to you?

Does career success mean earning a certain amount of money? Or does it mean securing a certain title? Does it mean having one or two direct reports or leading a large team? Or does it mean having autonomy in your role? Does it mean winning an industry award? Does it mean having a 50/50 work/life balance? Does it mean helping others in your work or contributing to the community? Does it mean being recognised as a subject-matter expert? Or does it mean being able to leave the office and switch off at 5pm Monday to Friday? Perhaps career success to you means not having to work on a weekend, or not having to answer to anyone in your role.

If you are just looking for a job, any job, in any industry, in any-sized company, in any location, that makes your search so much harder. You will be unfocused, using a scattergun approach where you try everything and anything to land any position. This means anyone you talk to won't really know what you want, and therefore they won't know how to help you.

This is why it's so important to get clear on what your dream, or ideal, role is.

In the following exercise, write down what would be the ideal environment/offering for you and then rank each item in order of importance using a scale of 1–10, with 'M' being a 'Must have' for your job satisfaction.

Dream Role

M = Must have   10 = High importance   1 = Low importance

Specific tangible factors

		Rank
Industry: (Same, similar or different?)		
Geographic location: (Location base, travel requirements, commuting requirements)		
Compensation package: (Base & bonus, profit sharing, options, equity)		
Benefits: (Training, health insurance, holidays, etc.)		
Company profile: (Size of company, growth, profitability)		
Position/goals: (Type of work, use of talents, promotion potential)		
Basis of promotion: (Merit, tenure)		

Intangible factors and 'nice to have'

	Rank
Company culture: (Management style, work climate, diversity of people)	
Lifestyle/work style: (White collar, open collar, flex-time, telecommuting)	
Type of boss: (Acts as teacher or mentor, allows freedom, gives feedback)	
Other: (Additional personal considerations)	

6. Achievements

Over the course of your career to date, you will have completed your job satisfactorily and there will also have been times when you went above and beyond what was expected of you. This may have resulted in specific results like saving the company money or time, streamlining systems or processes, or improving employee or customer satisfaction.

Ask yourself, "What did I do that made a difference?" Did you identify a wasteful procedure and recommend how to resolve it? Did you receive an award for something that you did particularly well? Did you achieve a great result despite budget cuts? Did you manage to lead your team and keep them motivated despite organisational change? Ask yourself these questions and more.

Any time your actions, or the actions you directed your team to take, resulted in a positive outcome for the company, you have an achievement. Use these items as prompts:

Identify your achievements

Situation – State a situation, issue or problem that you faced at work

Action – State the specific action/s you or you as a team leader or team member took to resolve this issue

Result – State the result of those actions in quantifiable terms if possible *(profit improvements, time savings, cost savings, perceived benefit to organisation, the 'value add')*

Now analyse the industry or company knowledge required to achieve this, the technical skills you used and also the personality traits that helped you to drive this to a successful outcome:

Knowledge

Skills

Personality traits

Achievement statement

Take the Action and the Result and turn it into a single sentence to describe this accomplishment for your resume. Accomplishment statements should be short, sharp and to the point, preferably starting with an action such as: Improved, Delivered, Streamlined, Reduced, Increased, Designed and Developed, Identified, and so on.

As a guide, here are three examples of achievement statements:

- *Improved staff communication, reward and recognition programs. This focus on individual development lifted staff engagement to employer of choice range (from 69% to 87% engagement score in the last financial year.)*

- *Developed and implemented multi channel campaigns to drive Membership Rewards program engagement. Resulted in growth in enrolment rates of 48% with average spend growth of 26% over 18 months.*
- *Led the successful development and implementation of an online Recruitment and Employee Change database, which streamlined and expedited the turnaround of approvals and commencement of recruitment, fast-tracking the on boarding of new recruits.*

Now it's your turn:

For additional support visit www.janejacksoncoach.com to download my free Job Search Guide and more valuable career resources too.

RESUMES AND YOUR MARKETING COMMUNICATIONS

"Skill in the art of communication is crucial to a leader's success. He can accomplish nothing unless he can communicate effectively."

– Anonymous

Now you know what's important to you in your career, it's time to set your communication strategy in place. This will take some time and concentrated effort; however, this preparation will be your foundation for success when you're ready to launch your job search and marketing campaign.

Before you make any job applications or start talking to people about the next step in your career, you need to do three things:

1. Craft and refine your verbal pitch or introduction.
2. Create your written marketing material (your resume and cover letters).
3. Set up your online profile via LinkedIn and optimise it for key word searches so potential employers or recruitment consultants can find you.

Without taking these three steps, you won't be able to market yourself effectively or credibly.

Verbal pitch

Who are you and what have you got to offer?

If you approach anyone regarding a job without knowing how to position yourself, you'll do yourself a disservice and you will waste a lot of time. Let's spend some time on your approach and what you are going to say.

You will need an introductory statement when speaking with recruitment consultants, potential hiring managers and with your general network. No one will know what you want and how he or she can help you if you are unclear when talking about yourself.

Most of my clients have told me that creating their introductory positioning statement is the hardest part of the job-search process. Why? Because most of us feel uncomfortable talking about ourselves when looking for a job. Many of my clients have told me that they don't want to sell themselves, they feel awkward and they don't like 'big noting' themselves. What about you? If you feel reluctance, too, all I can say is that if you don't express yourself clearly and let a potential hiring manager know what a great candidate you are, you won't get very far in the process! If you don't sell yourself, who's going to do it for you?

But don't fear – talking about your suitability for a role does not have to be a hard sell. It's about stating facts, highlighting the skills and experience that are relevant for the role, and letting your personality shine through.

The 60- to 90-second introduction

What would *you* say if someone said, "Tell me about yourself"?

The 60- to 90-second introduction is your answer. It is an important part of any networking meeting or interview. It provides an overview of what you have done and what you are looking for in a clear, concise and compelling capsule of information.

This introduction shares your employment background and aspirations, including your title, speciality and accomplishments, and also shares your current situation, which means your listener knows how they can help. Delivered well, your introduction can pique your listener's interest. And, at under 90 seconds, you will stay succinct and to the point.

When can you use a 90-second introduction?

- To respond to the question, "Tell me about yourself"
- During an informational interview/networking meeting
- At a pre-screening interview
- At a job interview
- In social situations
- Whenever there is an occasion to market yourself

These are opportunities to clearly articulate your career goals and, at the same time, create a positive, lasting impression with the listener.

So how do you do it? Here is a suggested format for the 60- to 90-second introduction:

Past experience (30–45 seconds)

Present the 'big picture' and your listener may ask you to elaborate on anything that is of interest. Include your most recent career history, an overview of the type of work you have been performing and the type of company, industry and functional experience you possess.

Current situation (about 15 seconds)

Here you explain why you are looking for work. Talk about this in a brief, matter-of-fact way and focus on the positive side of the change. It's important to have made the internal emotional transition so you are able to focus on the positives moving forward.

Future (about 30 seconds)

If in a networking meeting, talk about your target industry, position, function or role. Mentioning the names of organisations you are targeting or meeting with can be helpful. It is easier for people to make connections and offer support when they have specific information. If it is in an interview situation, focus on the skills and knowledge required for the role for which you are being interviewed.

Question

For example, "As you're familiar with the industry, in what other areas do you think there might be opportunities for a person with my experience?"

"In your experience, what do you consider to be the most critical skills in this area?"

"This role you have open sounds a close match to what I am looking for. I'm looking forward to learning more about it."

Asking a polite question promotes a two-way discussion. It is the component that will most likely change depending upon the reason you are using your Introduction.

Here's how to structure your introduction:

Past

I'm a sales manager with 8 years' experience in the manufacturing industry and extensive sales training experience, having led and mentored sales teams of up to 30. Most recently I was Sales Manager at Everest Manufacturing. My strengths are in creating and building new sales territories and relationship management. In my most recent role I grew the business by 40% within six months.

Current situation

You may be aware that, due to the merger with Summit Commercial Enterprises, there has been a duplication of roles and my position was made redundant. This has given me an opportunity to assess what I really want next in my career.

Future

I have a keen interest in sales, account management and developing sales teams. Leveraging my previous success in the manufacturing industry, I am now targeting global manufacturing companies that would benefit from my extensive Australian industry network and business development capabilities.

Question

With your experience in manufacturing here in Australia and overseas, I'd be interested to hear your thoughts and will appreciate any advice and suggestions you can give me.

Your introduction needs to be flexible – customised and responsive to the agenda and needs of the listener. This means your introduction will change depending on whether you are at a networking event, at an interview, or on the telephone. It is important to be able to expand your story when the opportunity presents itself, or to hold back if that is more appropriate.

As you've identified your values, your motivators, your skills and knowledge, and your achievements in the last chapter, you already have all the content you need to create a compelling verbal pitch.

To get started, simply follow this template.

Verbal pitch template

This template will help you to focus on the message you want to get across when asked at a networking meeting, "What do you do?" or "How can I help you?", or in an interview when you are asked, "So, tell me about yourself."

Networking

Past experience
I am a (profession) specialising in (*focus on your expertise, the industry or industries you have worked in*).

Current situation
Due to a recent restructure/due to my desire to explore (*explain what happened if you have left your previous company/explain why you are looking for a change if you are still in a role – make sure it is a non-emotional, factual statement*).

Future hopes
I'm now looking to leverage my experience and capabilities in (*mention what you would like to do moving forward*) and I am exploring (*be open to different directions where your listener may be able to guide you*).

Question to draw out more information
With your experience in   , I'd really appreciate your advice and guidance (*then ask a specific question to draw out the information you need*).

Interviewing

Past experience

I am a (*profession*) with experience in (*focus on your expertise, the industry or industries you have worked in*).

Most recently I have (*mention one of two relevant achievements that will demonstrate your suitability for the role you are inter- viewing for*).

Current situation

Due to a recent restructure/due to my desire to explore (*explain what happened if you have left your previous company/explain why you are looking for a change if you are still in a role – make sure it is a non-emotional, factual statement*).

Future hopes

I'm now keen to leverage my experience and capabilities in (*mention your relevant capabilities*) and this position you have open is of interest to me because (*mention the appeal of this role and how it ties in with your desired direction*).

Statement to draw out more information

I'm really interested to find out more about this company and this position.

Written marketing material – your resume and cover letters

Your resume

What's the role of a resume and what are the key points to remember when creating an effective one?

Let's take a few minutes to consider what happens to resumes. This will give you an understanding of how important it is to get your resume right before you send it out and why you need yours to really stand out.

A new job advertisement can elicit over hundreds of resumes. Depending on the size of an organisation and whether or not a company is using an agency or not for the recruitment process, your resume may or may not be read by a human being for the first cut. Many agencies use intelligent resume parsing technology, which eliminates the need for a consultant to trawl through hundreds of resumes. It provides a system that can be searched for particular candidate traits. What this means for you is that when you make an application your resume will be scanned automatically for key words that are reflected in the job ad. The system will then give your resume a percentage match. Resumes with a higher percentage match will most likely be read, and they will most likely be read first.

Even smaller organisations with talent acquisition team members who manually screen resumes work in a similar fashion – if the average recruitment consultant or HR consultant takes about 20 seconds to review each resume, that's three resumes per minute (without a break). To get through 200 resumes it would take over an hour. Multiply this by 6–8 positions, which is the average number of openings managed by a recruiter, and that's a lot of hours just for the initial screening and culling of resumes! This means that your resume needs to be immediately relevant to the position – otherwise it won't make the cut.

After resumes are screened, the screener goes through the selection to find resumes that fall into the categories of 'Yes' or 'Maybe'. The 'Yes' and 'Maybe' resumes will be given a more thorough reading after the initial screening. The 'No' resumes will be out.

Which resumes end up in the 'No' pile? Those that don't match those key words required for the role, those that have typographical errors, the resumes that are hard to follow, the ones with unexplained gaps in employment, the ones that don't address the selection criteria, the 'generic' resumes from candidates who simply send the same resume for every role without tailoring it to suit; none of these will make it through.

The odds of those candidates getting an email or an actual phone call thanking them for taking the time to apply are not very high. Some companies will respond to each and every applicant. Many don't.

If they do, often it's an automated response along the lines of 'We have received many applications from candidates who are a close match to our requirements and unfortunately you were not successful...'

So which resumes end up in the 'Yes' or 'Maybe' piles? Resumes make this cut for a number of reasons. Generally they are from candidates who were referred by another employee or were recommended by a friend (more on this in *Explore job search strategies that work*), and candidates whose resumes were the closest match to all the relevant key words in the job advertisement.

What can you do to maximise your chances of getting in to the pile of 'Yes' resumes so you continue in the selection process?

- Include a career summary or professional profile that highlights your relevant experience, core competencies and technical skills. This should capture the attention of the reader instantly.

How to Thrive When Changing Direction 69

- Make sure you are a fit for all of the 'must have' requirements of the role (and address each of these in your resume and cover letter!).
- Go through the job description carefully and use the key words from the advertisement in your career summary and in the body of your resume (providing you have those skills and aptitudes, of course!).
- Make sure your resume demonstrates the type of professional you are with the number of years of experience in specific industries or areas of specialisation – tailor this information to ensure you are a close match for the role for which you are qualified to apply.
- Remember to include accomplishments that highlight the additional value you brought to your current and previous roles.
- Choose a fuss-free layout and ensure your name and contact details (mobile phone and email address are requirements) are at the top.

Addressing each of these points will make it easy for the screener to see how close a match you are to the requirements of that specific role.

What to include in your resume

Contact details

These should be self-explanatory – your name, email address and mobile phone.

I suggest that you use your mobile phone number rather than a landline. This way you will be the one to answer the phone and avoid the possibility of getting a garbled message from someone else in your family. (One of my clients almost missed an opportunity because her son took a message and wrote down the wrong contact number.)

When setting up your email address, please be sure to make a professional sounding one. I've had one client use 'dirtywench@...' and another use 'mouseking@...' neither of which convey a corporate feel! Of course, if you're going for a role in an English pantomime then 'dirtywench@ ...' might be an attention grabber. It's up to you to decide what is, and what isn't, appropriate.

Career summary/professional profile

Your career summary or professional profile should highlight your relevant experience for the role, including your core competencies and technical skills. This is where you want to make use of key words and phrases from the advertisement to quickly get the screener's attention.

I'd recommend that you write this in third person rather than in first person, and make it short, sharp and to the point. For example, rather than writing, "I am a highly skilled and results-oriented Sales Manager with extensive experience in the pharmaceutical industry and, over the past eight years, have progressed from ..." change it to something like, "Results-driven Sales Manager with extensive experience within the pharmaceutical industry. A specialist in ... Highly skilled in ..."

It's a small adjustment; however, it gets straight to the point. Remember, screeners may have to review dozens or hundreds of resumes, so make it easy for them to find what they are looking for. Make sure you capture their attention right from the start by being relevant to the specific role you're applying for.

Professional experience

Your professional experience should include company names, a brief description of the business, job titles, the dates you held each role, the scope of the role and your achievements while in the role. (Review exercise 6 on page 58 in *Assess what makes you tick* to learn how to craft an effective achievement statement.)

Academic qualifications/personal development

Any relevant academic qualifications and professional development courses have their own section in the resume, too. Include your qualifications or certifications, as well as the institutions or examining bodies that granted each one.

Memberships/associations

Include any memberships/associations that are relevant to the role. This is especially important as it demonstrates that you are keeping active in your area of specialisation. Of course, I expect you will be joining associations to become an active member, and not just to put it on your resume! Whether you are an engineer, CPA, project manager or coach, there may be an association or body that you can join where you will be able to socialise with like-minded professionals with whom you can share ideas, network and learn something new.

Referees

In an initial application, referees can be 'available upon request'. You don't need to put them in if you don't wish to as we all know that, should you progress to reference check stage, you will then be asked to provide referee contact details.

If the job advertisement specifically requests referee details, then follow the application instructions.

Layout and presentation

How long should your resume be? Please keep it to 2–3 pages; no one wants to read a long, rambling dissertation on your entire work/life history. The most relevant information will be from the last 10–12 years so place the most focus on that time period.

The key thing about formatting is to make sure it's easy to read – there is no point in squeezing a lengthy tome on to two pages in 8-point font with very narrow margins! No one will want to read it – especially those people, like me, who have to get out their reading glasses for anything smaller than 10-point font. A font size of 10–12 point is user-friendly. Ensuring decent margin widths and enough white space, also improves readability. Remember that screeners look for any reason NOT to read a resume, especially if there are hundreds of applicants, so don't get caught out on formatting.

Finally, proofread, proofread, and proofread!!! Get someone else to proofread it, too – sometimes you can work so hard on your resume that you don't even notice the little mistakes any more. Spelling and grammatical errors in a resume show a lack of attention to detail and you won't get very far in the application process. One executive search firm executive told me that if he spotted a spelling error he'd reject that application immediately. If an application for a specific role is important enough to you, there should be no silly mistakes.

Functional versus reverse-chronological resumes

Most screeners (especially recruiters) prefer a reverse-chronological resume. That means that your resume focuses on your most recent role, your responsibilities and achievements in that role, and then it goes back in time. This resume is preferred as it is easy to see what position you held and which industry and size of company you've worked in on page one of your resume. Most recruitment consultants prefer to put forward candidates who have recent relevant experience that is a match to the role they need to fill. This applies to their functional capability, the level they worked at, their industry experience and the size of organisation they have worked in.

A functional resume lists your capabilities before going into your work experience. This type of resume is sometimes viewed with suspicion, as the screener may think you are trying to hide something, like a patchy career history or lack of recent relevant experience. However, if you are looking to make a career change and you want to highlight your capabilities rather than your recent roles, then the functional format is an option. If want to go back to something that you did a number of years ago, but your career took a different path for a while, the functional resume will give you the chance to demonstrate your capabilities before the reader sees where you've worked most recently.

Resume templates

Here are two templates for you to consider: the reverse-chronological format and the functional format.

Reverse-chronological resume template

YOUR NAME
Email:
Mobile:

PROFESSIONAL PROFILE
Insert your positioning statement tailored for the role you are targeting

PROFESSIONAL EXPERIENCE

| **COMPANY NAME** | **CITY** | **DATE–DATE** |

Brief description of business

Job Title   Date–Date
Reported to …
Responsible for …

Achievements
- Developed ...
- Streamlined ...

Job Title Date–Date

Reported to ...

Responsible for ...

Achievements
- Led the team to ...
- Successfully delivered ...

COMPANY NAME **CITY** **DATE–DATE**

Brief description of business

Job Title Date–Date

Reported to ...

Responsible for ...

Achievements
- Designed and developed ...
- Analysed ...

ACADEMIC QUALIFICATIONS AND PROFESSIONAL DEVELOPMENT

Qualification

University or examining body

Certification

Examining body

MEMBERSHIPS/ASSOCIATIONS

Membership

Functional resume template

YOUR NAME
Email:
Mobile:

PROFESSIONAL PROFILE

Insert your positioning statement tailored for the role you are targeting.

FUNCTIONAL CAPABILITIES

e.g., Business development/strategic planning
Developed ...
Streamlined ...

e.g., Project management
Led the team to ...
Delivered ...

e.g., Training and development
Designed and developed ...
Facilitated ...

PROFESSIONAL EXPERIENCE

COMPANY NAME	**CITY**	**DATE–DATE**
Brief description of business		
Job Title		Date–Date
Job Title		Date–Date
COMPANY NAME	**CITY**	**DATE–DATE**
Brief description of business		
Job Title		Date–Date

ACADEMIC QUALIFICATIONS AND PROFESSIONAL DEVELOPMENT

Qualification

University or examining body

Certification

Examining body

MEMBERSHIPS/ASSOCIATIONS

Membership

Cover letters

Whenever you make an application, more often than not you will also be asked to provide a cover letter. But does it really make a difference?

To be honest, from talking to many human resources professionals and recruiters, the response is about 50/50 as to whether or not a cover letter is important.

Many have told me that they go straight to the resume, as they don't want to read 'fluff'.

Many have told me that they always read a cover letter, as the letter will highlight the reason why someone is applying for the role and also will demonstrate how well they write.

This is why correct grammar, spelling and layout are so important. Make it easy for the reader to see that you are an ideal candidate for the role, and that you have what it takes to be successful. Even if only 50% of recruiters and hiring managers read the cover letter, for those 50% it is essential to get it right.

Here is a sample template that you can follow if you are stuck when it comes to writing cover letters. Remember that a cover letter should be no longer than one page and what you include must be relevant to the reader.

Sample cover letter

Dear *(Mr/Ms Surname)*,

*(make sure you have the correct name – DO **NOT** PUT 'TO WHOM IT MAY CONCERN')*

Re: Job title, reference number, date advertised and where found

I'm writing in response to your advertisement for a *(role/title)* in *(source of advertisement)* on *(date)* as I believe my background, skills and experience are well matched to the requirements of the role.

My current/most recent experience is as a *(role)* at *(name of company)* and my core areas of responsibility are/have been *(include the four or five areas targeted by the advertisement)*, which I believe relate directly to the requirements of the advertised role. In particular, the following capabilities are relevant to your requirements:

Xxx

Xxx

Xxx

(Mention the difference that you will be able to make to the organisation, the value you will add in addition to what is stated in the job description. You will need to conduct research to ensure what you mention is relevant.)

With your recent acquisition of XYZ Company and the need for expertise in change management, my experience in leading teams through organisational change will be of immediate benefit.

(Mention the attachments that may have been requested)

> I attach the following in support of my application:
> - Resume
> - Response to Selection Criteria
>
> I look forward to the opportunity to discuss this role further with you in an interview.
>
> Yours sincerely,
>
> *(Sign off with name, mobile number and email contact)*

Providing referees

At some stage in the job-search process you will be asked for the names and contact details of your referees. If you have ever been in a position to hire someone in the past, you'll know the challenges when getting the real story about their past performance. This is why employers carefully check references to find out as much as they can about past performance before making an offer. Reference checks are part of their due diligence before confirming a job offer.

What are employers looking for when conducting a reference check?

1. Employers need to find out if what is in the resume and what was discussed during the interview process is true.
2. Companies need legal protection in case someone has had a history of violence or crime. If there have been problems in the past that might cause harm or discomfort to colleagues or customers, this may turn out to be more than just a bad hire – it might turn out to be the target of a lawsuit.
3. Hiring managers want to hire someone who is able to hit the ground running. Past performance is an indicator of future success so the accurate confirmation of accomplishments is important.

4. Psychological fit is so important as hiring managers know that employees who fit with the company and team culture will get along with colleagues more easily than if they are not a good fit.
5. The reference check stage is a good time for the caller to pick up on subtle clues,to read between the lines as to the suitability of a candidate.

Provide at least two referees to the potential employer or recruitment consultant. Most recruiters prefer to be given the names and contact details of two previous managers. You may provide more referees if you wish. Make sure that you include a brief description of your relationship under each referee's contact details (e.g., 'Reported to John Smith between 2012 and 2014' or 'Reported to Jack Black when he was Group Finance Director 2010–2012').

When putting together your list of referees, use the following template:

YOUR NAME
Mobile:
Email:

REFEREES

1. **Name**
   Title (current)
   Company (current)
   Phone:
   Email:

   Brief description of relationship (e.g., Reported to... when in the role of ... during the period ... dates)

2. **Name**
   Title (current)
   Company (current)
   Phone:
   Email:

   Brief description of relationship

3. **Name**
   Title (current)
   Company (current)
   Phone:
   Email:

   Brief description of relationship

LinkedIn and online branding

The job market is moving online, from both a recruiter and a candidate perspective, so you need to get your online presence organised if you're going to make the most of this opportunity.

I've had clients who refuse to use social media as they prefer to remain private. I respect that, however, when it comes to the job search process, consider this: 94% of recruiters are using social media for recruiting, according to a Jobvite Social Recruiting survey. Additionally, employers who use social media to hire have found a 49% improvement in candidate quality over candidates sourced only through traditional recruiting channels.

2018 LinkedIn statistics show that it is the world's largest online professional network with over 640 million members in over 240 countries and territories, including over 10 million members in Australia. Around 90% of all recruiters report having hired someone through LinkedIn, according to Herd Wisdom, and 94 of the Fortune 100 companies use LinkedIn's corporate talent solutions.

90 million LinkedIn users are senior level influencers, and 63 million are in decision making positions.

What about from the candidate perspective? While 94% of recruiters are active on LinkedIn, only 36% of candidates are, according to Jobvite. This means there is an abundance of opportunity just waiting for you to tap into.

As one of my clients told me recently, "I was surprised how many recruiters contacted me when my LinkedIn profile was used as an informative tool!"

LinkedIn is a professional networking site that enables members to interact with their connections, conduct research on companies, look for jobs advertised by other members and to find out who, within their network of connections, could potentially provide a link to a hiring manager in their target company.

Creating a LinkedIn profile and knowing how to interact with your connections is not difficult; however, I've found that many of my clients aren't using LinkedIn as effectively as they could simply because they haven't taken the time to explore the functionality of the platform. This site is for professional networking. The information you include in your profile, or omit from your profile, will affect your professional brand online.

This professional online network is a great place to showcase your achievements and build a network of professional contacts. As in all business situations, following the correct etiquette will ensure you present yourself in the most positive light.

Go on to www.linkedin.com, sign up for a free account and set up your profile. You can pay to upgrade your profile for added functionality however the free version is perfectly effective to initially manage your online brand.

Here are a few tips that will guide you as you decide what to include, what not to include and what to do with your profile once it's complete. LinkedIn is constantly evolving and improving so make sure that you use the help function on the site and you may discover new offerings as time goes on.

Include a profile picture

As this is the first thing people notice when they visit your LinkedIn profile, use a professional-looking photo that reflects what you represent.

For example, if you are the male CEO of a financial services organisation, it would make sense to have a professional photo taken wearing a well-tailored suit, shirt and tie. If you are the creative director of an advertising agency, you will want to represent yourself in a less formal and more creative light. An image consultant would want to highlight his or her ability to use colour that enhances his or her skin tone and create a striking, vibrant, co-ordinated profile photo.

Always ensure that you look at the camera, your eyes can be seen and you have a smile or a positive expression on your face. Hint: Head-and-shoulders shots work best for LinkedIn.

I've seen a lot of profile photos that have made me wonder what the user was thinking when uploading their shot, so here are a few suggestions so you upload a great photo and do yourself justice!

Dos and don'ts of LinkedIn profile photos

Do	Don't
Ensure your head and shoulders fill the photo	Stand too far away in a full-length shot
Ensure the photo is clear and well lit	Use a dimly lit and fuzzy photo
Choose a plain background	Choose a distracting background
Dress for the role you want	Use a casual, holiday snap
Use a professional photographer	Crop a photo with others in it
Smile	Have an unfriendly expression
Ensure your eyes are visible	Look away or close your eyes
Project your professional image	Wear sunglasses

Professional photographer, Peter Morris of Sydney Heads, whose work has been featured in The New York Times, The Independent (London) and Sydney Morning Herald advises, *"First impressions count. A great LinkedIn profile photo is like a visual handshake. The key 'look' is confidence with approachability."*

Complete your profile

Add a tagline under your name, add an 'About' section, add professional experience, your significant accomplishments, website address, awards, and memberships, and so on. You can also add sections to include the business books you are reading, promote events you're hosting or attending, and highlight your blog or any articles in publications you have had published.

Your tagline

Your tagline is an important element in your profile, as this is what people will see first under your name. LinkedIn automatically fills this in for you and defaults to your most recent job title and company name. You can change it easily using the 'edit' function.

You'll notice that many people don't bother to change their tagline (or aren't aware that they can). It's an important part of your LinkedIn real estate so don't waste it with a job title that doesn't describe what you have to offer.

For example, Senior Consultant at ABC Company or Associate at XYZ Finance doesn't tell you much. However, a tagline like, "Sales and Telesales Trainer | Speaker | Sales Strategist | Author" immediately lets us know that this person is a sales specialist, published author and one who is able to train others in the subject.

As another example, "Business Transformation| Process Migration Specialist | Project Manager (PMP, PRINCE2 & ITIL)" lets us know that this is a certified project manager able to assist us with business process migration.

My tagline states: "Career Management Coach | LinkedIn Trainer | Personal Branding | Resume Coach | Author | Podcast Host" because these key words cover the services I provide.

This ensures my profile has a chance of showing up if someone is seeking a professional with any of those skill sets.

Your 'About' section

There is great debate about the 'About' secction, so I'll share my recommendations and you can make up your mind as to what works best for you. Some people like to cut and paste the summary or profile (which will be in the third person, sharp and to the point) from their resume verbatim. While that could work for you, here's my take on it: LinkedIn is social media. It's a professional networking site and therefore people want to get to know you. Therefore I believe that the 'About' section in your LinkedIn profile should be in the first person. Your reader should feel that they are getting to know you and the way you work when they read 'About' you. Make it interesting so that you stand out and are memorable!

For example, while searching LinkedIn I found a profile with an 'About' section that spoke so well about this person:

"It's one thing to have solid skills; e.g., being a coach or trainer, but running a successful coaching or training business is a whole different ball game!

I have over 14 years of sales and managerial experience, plus have experienced first-hand the challenges and rewards of being a start-up business. I eventually left the corporate world and co-founded my second venture XXX to pursue my mission and passion – to inspire, empower, educate and enable entrepreneurs to achieve personal and professional success.

If you are an entrepreneur who's been struggling to find your way, or a budding superstar looking to transition to becoming your own boss, I am here to help. Having been on both sides of the equation, I am eager to share my life experiences and offer mentoring and guidance to help others follow in my footsteps."

Reading this, I can feel this person's enthusiasm and passion. What will your 'About' section evoke?

Give and receive recommendations

Request recommendations from business contacts, as these lend credibility to your profile. If someone in a position of authority provides you with a recommendation, it strengthens your profile.

LinkedIn allows you to request recommendations from your connections. Simply go to the profile of the person whom you'd like to provide a recommendation on LinkedIn and on the top right you will see a tab that says, "More ..." Click that and you will see an option that says "Request a recommendation" Click that and follow the prompts. If you are not able to find a function you are looking for on LinkedIn, please use the 'help' function to assist you.

When choosing someone to recommend you, previous managers are an obvious choice, as are clients and colleagues who can vouch for the way that you work and how effective you are in your role. When someone recommends you, it will show up on their profile, too, unless they choose to hide the recommendation.

Of course you can recommend others you know and respect, too. This is a lovely gesture to show your recognition of their talent and always very much appreciated. You can use the Settings feature to show the recommendations you make on your profile, or you can choose to hide them. The choice is yours.

One thing to remember is that a 'tit for tat' recommendation dilutes the effectiveness of any recommendation. Please don't take the attitude of trying to rake up a high number of recommendations simply by telling colleagues that you'll recommend them if they recommend you. Work with integrity and be genuine when making or receiving any recommendations.

Join groups

Another way to connect with people on LinkedIn is by joining groups, as LinkedIn allows you to connect with people who are in the same group as you. To join groups that are relevant to your industry or job function, simply type in a topic of interest in the search field at the top of your LinkedIn page and you will find a list of related groups. Click on each one to find out more about them and how many members there are. Some of the groups will also let you see who their members are and the group's discussions before you become a member. If there are intelligent discussions on your area of specialisation and/or people of interest in the group, this may be a group you'd like to join.

Simply click on the 'Join' button and either you will automatically be a member or, in some cases, an administrator will have to approve your membership. You can always leave a group later if you change your mind by going into your settings and following the links in the Groups, Companies & Applications section.

The beauty of groups is that you can post comments and start discussions on your area of interest and like-minded professionals will be alerted to your presence. You will also learn from others and their discussions.

I've had a lot of fun and interesting discussions with other coaches when I have posted comments or created my own discussions on career management topics. Give it a go and see what happens! I can guarantee that it will result in, at the very least, more people viewing your profile to see who you are.

Post regular status updates

Post status updates on your *area of expertise* that will add value to your audience in a specific industry or sector. Updating your LinkedIn status makes you pop up in the news feed of your connections and reminds them of what you have to offer. This is an excellent PR activity.

On your home page or news feed there is a field at the top of the page where you can add a link or publish a post (your own articles). LinkedIn is rolling out the publishing capability to all members, so if you haven't got it yet, you will soon or you can make contact via the help function and request for publishing status. Even if you can't publish a post you've written at present, you can always attach links to interesting articles in your areas of expertise or links to blog posts you have written on your own website.

Every time you turn up on your connections' news feed they will be reminded of who you are and what you offer. I always post articles or attach links to information about job search, communication skills, career transition, professional image, coaching or building self-confidence, as these are the services I offer. Therefore, every time someone sees my posts, they are reminded that I am a career coach.

#LinkedInLive

If you type the word LinkedInLive with a hashtag # at the beginning, in the search field on LinkedIn you will find many past 'live' video broadcasts on LinkedIn. At the time of writing, LinkedIn is rolling this out to a few beta testers across the world and as time goes by more people will have access. The beauty of #LinkedInLive is that specialists in their field can educate, entertain and communicate with the LinkedIn audience in real time.

I am a beta tester for this #LinkedInLive facility and provide 'live' job search tips. To view my past live videos, use this hashtag: #askjanecareercoach

The beauty of #linkedinlive is that you are broadcasting 'live' to the entire world. Everyone can tap into your message in real-time or they have the opportunity to watch the replay and comment too.

With hundreds of millions of members at the touch of a keyboard, the power of this facility is mind boggling. To see if you have access, go to your Home page on Linkedin (on your laptop or computer) and see if, on the left hand side, there is a section that says 'Linkedin Live' – if there is, you can apply to receive access to this a facility, if not, you will need to wait until LinkedIn rolls it out to you too.

Tailor your invitations to connect

When inviting someone to connect, please personalise your message. It's almost rude not to and is a sign of laziness to send a generic invitation.

If you look at my 'About' section on my profile at www.linkedin.com/in/janejackson you will read exactly what you need to say when requesting to connect with me.

Any time I receive a generic request I know that person has NOT read my profile otherwise they would have followed instructions!

I do this because I receive many requests to connect from LinkedIn users who are simply collecting numbers. I believe in quality over quantity - networking requires a personal connection.

Always make the effort to get to know your connections as this is a professional networking platform.

Let's connect!

Connect with me on LinkedIn – and remember to provide a personalised message (if you read my 'About' section on my profile I tell you what to say when making a connection request!) www.linkedin.com/in/janejackson

Follow companies of interest

Search for companies, via the search field at the top of the webpage, that are on your target list and click on 'follow'. You will then receive regular company updates on your home page – new developments, when they are hiring, people on the move, and so on.

Don't forget to check your spelling and grammar

Just as you would proofread your resume before sending it out, ensure you proofread your profile before making it visible to all.

Don't add people you don't know

If you request a connection to a stranger, you will devalue the real connections you have. Add only the people you truly have a connection with. You can send invitations to connect with someone on LinkedIn simply by clicking on the 'Connect' button

if you know their email address, or you know someone who knows them (i.e., a 2nd connection). If you don't know someone who knows that person, then it gets trickier. I don't recommend connecting to people you don't know and have never met, plus have no connection to link you together. What's the point? If you connect with anyone and everyone, I believe it's a bit like junk mail – most people put little value on it.

I believe a networking site is to make connections with people with whom you have something in common and would like to keep in touch. It reinforces the relationship and generates a feeling of trust. Therefore, I connect only with those with whom I have worked in a professional capacity or have met personally. The only times I have connected with people I have not met personally is when I have interacted electronically to find out more about them, or have been personally recommended to them by someone I know. This way, if a client of mine asks me if I am able to make an introduction to one of my connections, I am able to do so in the knowledge that I will very likely get a positive response. If I am connected to people who don't know me, it's as good as a cold call.

This topic generates great debate so the call is yours to make. But, when it comes to quality versus quantity, I'd go with quality every time.

Don't bombard your connections

The key is consistency and posting quality updates that are of interest to your target audience. I usually post once every day or so and publish a blog post related to careers and coaching once a week.

Post frequently enough so that you get noticed without overdoing it. I've seen some connections post 4–5 times every day and then I tend not to read those updates as I feel overloaded! However, if you post too infrequently then you also run the risk of not being noticed, as your activity update gets pushed further down everyone's news feed. Be sensible about your updates.

When you do publish a post, or write an article on your area of expertise, make sure the heading is a compelling one that will generate interest. I was pleasantly surprised when an article I posted one Saturday morning entitled, "Do you appear desperate when following up?" generated over 49,000 views, over 200 comments and over 1,700 shares within one week. This also resulted in numerous emails asking about my coaching services and was a great boost for my business and visibility. The article heading must have touched a nerve and word spread through all the 'shares' that post received.

Enjoy updating your profile and conducting your research to enhance your job search activities – LinkedIn is a great resource so manage your online brand effectively!

Have a look at my public profile – you'll see the additional sections and applications you can add to enhance your own profile too: http://www.linkedin.com/in/janejackson.

How to ensure your profile is optimised for search

Most people don't realise how the LinkedIn search function works. It is driven by key words. This means that, if you want your profile to turn up for a recruiter or a hiring manager looking for someone like you, you must include all the relevant key words in your profile so that you will turn up in a search.

For example, if you are a marketing manager and you focus on specific categories and channel marketing within the pharmaceutical industry, you must include those key words in your profile, in both the summary section as well as in the experience section in your profile.

For example, have a look at the **bold** words in this summary – this profile came up top of my search when I experimented with those key words:

*"I am a results-driven **marketing** professional with over 15 years' experience in handling OTC **pharmaceuticals**, consumer packaged and consumer durable brands. I have an extensive and proven track record in the fields of Brand Management, **Channel/Trade Marketing, and as a category lead** with sound exposure in business development and sales.*

*I work around the simplest of **marketing** philosophies – knowing both consumers and shoppers intimately so that the right drivers are activated and the products I market fit them perfectly.*

*Specialties: Brand Management, **Channel/Trade Marketing**, New Product Development and Launches, Integrated **Marketing** Campaigns, Creative Media Planning, and Below-the-Line activation, Consumer/Shopper Insight generation, Market Research and Business Analytics."*

Think about what your key words should be and, if you have experience or exposure in those areas, please make sure you include those words in your summary and experience.

If you want to know how you rank in the number of profile views compared to others in your field on LinkedIn, you will need to upgrade your free profile to a premium profile. You can do this in the Settings section of your profile. With an upgraded profile you will also be able to see how people were led to your profile

– whether it was by a specific search for your name, a search for professionals in your industry or other search criteria.

While upgrading your account can be helpful, even without having to pay for a premium account, LinkedIn is a highly effective way to be found and conduct research on companies, other professionals in your area of expertise and industry and to look for jobs.

How to use LinkedIn for research

LinkedIn is a great resource to find out about companies and also to find the people who work in those companies.

For example, if you are interested in targeting Adecco in Australia, type in the search field at the top of your LinkedIn page the words 'Adecco Australia'.

The company page will open and you will see all the information that Adecco posts on LinkedIn about the company, careers and recent updates, and you can click on the 'follow' button to receive regular updates from them.

You will also see how many employees from Adecco have LinkedIn profiles and how you are connected to those people. The company page shows you how many Adecco employees are connected to you directly (1st degree connections) and how many employees you are connected to through someone you already know (2nd degree connections).

What this means for you is that you can easily find out via LinkedIn whom you can approach for an introduction to someone within that company. It makes the networking process quicker and much easier than if you had to work through your entire list of contacts to find out whom they know in various companies.

For example, one of my connections told me, "When I went for my last job I looked on LinkedIn to see who I knew at the company. It turned out I had two 2nd degree connections, one of whom was the former Marketing Manager. (I was going for a job in the marketing team.) I asked our shared contact for an introduction, explaining that I was going for a job at the company and wanted to learn more about it before my interview. Our shared connection made the introduction, and I ended up getting a coffee with the former Marketing Manager who shared a lot of insights into how the company was structured, who I'd be interviewed by (as well as what to expect and how to interact with them), who I'd be working with if I got the job, and potential issues that might come up."

From a personal perspective, I was recently recommended to connect with a journalist by one of my group workshop participants. Rather than send a request to connect directly to that journalist, I sent a request for an introduction via LinkedIn to my workshop participant and he contacted that journalist directly with his endorsement. Having the endorsement of another person who is in your target's sphere of influence more often than not opens doors.

When using LinkedIn for research, do you want people to know you've viewed their profile?

This is always a topic of great debate when discussing LinkedIn and research. If you use the default settings in LinkedIn, when you view someone's profile, depending on whether they are using the free version or have upgraded their profile, they may be able to see that you have viewed their profile.

The benefit of someone knowing that you've viewed their profile is that it alerts them to your presence if you want to be noticed. Also, if you are going to be interviewed by that person soon, they will know that you are doing your due diligence by preparing and conducting research prior to the interview.

If you are just looking at profiles out of curiosity and don't wish to be identified, there is the option to be anonymous. In order to change the default setting, go to the top right of your LinkedIn page and click on the icon (usually your photo) and in the drop-down menu click on "Privacy & Settings", then choose "Select what others see when you've viewed their profile". Here you can decide how visible you wish to be.

How to use LinkedIn for job applications

LinkedIn also has an excellent job search function. All you need to do is to type in the sort of position you are looking for in the search (for example 'operations manager, mining, Perth') and jobs with those key words will pop up. You will also see people with the key words 'operations manager, mining and Perth' in their profiles, whom you could approach for advice and guidance.

If you seek a role in a specific city, type that city in the search field. LinkedIn also allows you to search for remote roles where you may work from home, or from anywhere in the world. Type in the search field, "Remote" and see what pops up.

When you see a role that looks interesting, click on it and you will see the job description. There will be a link to the company or recruiter's website where you can apply. You may also see the name and link to the profile of the person who posted the job. This could be a hiring manager, internal talent acquisition specialist or a recruiter.

This means that you can apply for the role and also make contact with the person who posted the role to direct them to your LinkedIn profile. It gives you an additional 'touch point' that may help to progress your application.

There is so much that you can do on LinkedIn; even more as LinkedIn continues to improve its customer experience. Keep up to date by logging on regularly and exploring the updates and changes so that you stay on top of the benefits provided.

EXPRESS YOUR PERSONAL BRAND AND PROFESSIONAL IMAGE

"Your image is nine-tenths of success."

– Loren Fogelman, Author
The Winning Point: How to Master the Mindset of Champions

When it comes to looking for a job, have you ever wondered why, when qualifications and experience are equal, some people gain an advantage over their competitors? Often it's not because they are any better qualified for the job, but because they present themselves as if they were. They create the impression that they are a good fit for the role and the culture of the organisation. The positive first impression they project paves the way to their success.

Your personal presentation will undermine or establish your credibility. If you are lacking, it brings your credibility into question. By contrast, if you project a positive first impression it will pave your way and make things easier when developing any relationship.

I remember meeting, for the first time, the senior partner of a consulting company one morning at her office. She was dressed quite casually with a cardigan and comfortable pants and I mistook her for a junior office member. When I found out who she was I was surprised; my initial impression was that her approach would be rather casual, too, and I wondered about how effective and professional she'd be. As it turned out, she was sharp as a tack, totally professional in her approach, but it took me a while to realise this as I'd formed my first impression of her and my assumptions needed to be turned around. Can you remember a time when you've made an assumption as to the competence, professionalism or ability of someone simply from the initial visual impression?

First impressions do count. If you make a polished and professional entrance, it will ease your way as you will have set the bar at that level. If you set the bar low, it will take longer to prove how good you are. We're all human – we're judgemental and we assume things very quickly, whether they are correct or not.

However, your image is not just what you wear. Your image is not all visual. Your image needs to be considered from five angles.

There are five essential components of your image that come together and affect the way others perceive you. Consider your:

1. Hidden image
2. Assumed image
3. Visual image
4. Experienced image
5. Proven image over time

Your hidden image

Your hidden image encompasses what you believe about yourself, your past experiences and any fears that may be holding you back. Whether you were first born, second born or the baby of the family plays a part in how you view your world, along with whether you are male or female, whether you had an easy childhood or if your early life was a struggle, and more.

Others won't be able to see this hidden image, and you can't see the hidden image of others, but it affects what we see, hear, do and how we react to every situation every day.

So how does this affect your job search? From my experiences and those of the clients I have coached over the past 14 years, our hidden image plays the trump card when it comes to success and the way we handle challenges.

For example, one of my clients came to me in 2001 full of angst and anger after losing her job as a senior finance manager in a company where she'd worked for over 15 years. Her choices had been strongly influenced by the expectations of her parents who had wanted to have a finance professional in the family. She was a dutiful daughter and had complied, as she was quite good at mathematics, statistics and economics at school and at university. However, what she really enjoyed was something quite different, but that was never an option for her as a career path while she followed the expectations and assumptions of her family.

The culture in which she'd been brought up meant that a daughter was expected to do the 'right thing', to be deferential to her parents, and to do as she was told. In the early days she didn't know anything different – it was just the way things were. While there is nothing wrong with that, however, this was not making her happy.

I met her at a career crossroads. She was angry, resentful, fed up and told me that she hated finance. She didn't want to be a finance manager. She didn't want to be in corporate life. She didn't want to have to answer to a manager for whom she had no respect. She'd felt stuck for a long time, doing what was considered the right thing, and she was miserable.

She was also afraid about the future as she simply didn't know what to do.

During our coaching sessions we discovered that she had a lot of passion within – she had hopes and dreams and unfulfilled desires for herself and her career, which she was almost afraid to admit. She wasn't quite sure of how to harness those hopes and dreams until one day we were talking about what would make her heart sing. She opened up and told me about her involvement with the local wine and food society. When she spoke (with great authority) about wine, cheese, specialty foods and all things gourmet she was a different person. No longer did I see the angry, resentful, frustrated finance manager; instead, I saw the eager, excited, brightly lit foodie!

Needless to say, this exploration led to much angst and debate about what would be the 'right thing' to do moving forward with family expectations and self-limiting beliefs. However, she bit the bullet and took herself off on a number of gastronomic tours of Tuscany and Tasmania, exploring and coming up with a number of wild and wonderful ideas for another business.

After much research, number crunching (it was useful that she was good at finance after all), negotiating with potential investors, gaining a reliable business partner and fantastic venue, she launched her own business – a fabulous restaurant that has now been in business for over 10 years.

It took a lot of hard work and there was much to overcome with the way she perceived the world from her upbringing, her hidden image, her personal goals and her hidden expectations and beliefs about herself.

However, I'm delighted to say that she is now a successful businesswoman with a very successful business, she answers to herself and her customers, she is a motivating manager and leader, has become the most amazing chef along the way and she knows everything about wine, cheese and everything gourmet!

Think about your hidden image – what are your expectations, what are the expectations of your family and friends, how does that affect your choices and the way you view your world and how does it affect your job search?

Your assumed image

We are all pre-conditioned to develop expectations about a person even before we meet them. Our first impression depends a lot on what we've heard about them, what we think we already know.

What is their reputation in their industry? How are they portrayed on social media? Who do they work for? What position do they hold? Which country are they from? What social demographic were they brought up in? Depending on what we know, we will expect them to behave in a certain way, hold certain beliefs and communicate in a certain way. The same is true when it comes to what others expect of us.

Do you know what people expect before they meet you? Do you represent your brand accurately? In your current or previous role, did you measure up to the expectations of new clients or new staff members when they met you?

Last year the Managing Partner of a law firm asked me to provide a 60-minute presentation on professional image to her associates to be broadcast across Australia to all their offices. I was surprised when she told me that she was not happy with the way the lawyers were presenting themselves when meeting clients. She told me that they did not represent the image of the firm well and it was harming their standing in the industry.

I had always assumed that lawyers would naturally present themselves in a 'lawyer-like' fashion. Now what is 'lawyer-like' you may ask? My initial expectation would be a dark, well-tailored, suit, beautiful leather accessories, impeccably cut business shirt, expensive shoes and discreet jewellery. Now, that is my view of the legal world. It may be different from yours. However, if a lawyer does not present in that visual fashion during a business meeting, I (rightly or wrongly) would assume that they might not be up to scratch.

Another example of assumed image is that if my daughter needed the assistance of a doctor in an emergency ward, I'd more readily hand her over to someone in a clean white coat than someone in blue jeans and a t-shirt (even if his or her name tag stated that he or she was a specialist) simply because I assume a doctor should dress a certain way when on duty.

Fair or not, remember – you never know whom you will be meeting and what their expectations and assumptions of you will be. If you want to present a positive impression to your target audience, be aware of how you are perceived and the expectations that others have of you in your profession, at your level, in your industry.

Your visual image

Your visual image is how you physically present yourself, including what you wear and your body language.

In a work environment, how you dress affects how professional you look, along with your posture, eye contact, smiles and nods. These all create a visual image, or personal brand, from which people make judgements about your professionalism, abilities and more.

Russell's story

Russell was in his 50s when he was made redundant after 35 years in a stable government job. In the eyes of younger employees, he was already seen as an 'old man', and some of them referred to him as one of 'The Greys'.

While he eventually found another position, he felt that if he'd paid more attention to his visual image, he could have found one much sooner.

"I think that initially I was too open with what I said to others and not as sensitive to other points of view. I should have taken steps earlier to become savvy to the new world I was in. I realised that I needed to make friends with the younger people and learn about the new technologies to stay current. I bought myself an up-to-date laptop and, over time, an iPad, an iPhone and got up to speed with the new ways of doing things.

"I also would have updated my visual image earlier, too. I found that in order to be taken seriously I couldn't look like an 'old man' and I took steps to dress age-appropriately but with a current feel."

So how can you tailor your visual image? The first step is reviewing your wardrobe.

When it comes to what to wear in an interview or business setting, expectations will vary depending on the organisation you represent. A lawyer or chief financial officer will not be expected to dress like the creative director from an advertising agency or the showroom manager of a fashion PR company.

If your appearance surprises, people will try to make sense of it and may come to an inaccurate conclusion. If you want to impress certain groups of people and create a positive impression, their reactions will be shaped by a whole range of beliefs (their own hidden image), which make them more, or less, receptive to you and what you represent.

So what should you wear for business success? If you are at a loss, here is a simple guide when setting up a basic business wardrobe.

The basics of a professional woman's wardrobe

- 1 x suit dress (black – double up as Little Black Dress)
- 2 x tailored plain black pants
- 2 x black pencil skirts
- 1 x black suit jacket

- 1 × suit jacket – charcoal, red, royal blue, cream, black and white, or speckle – choose a colour that suits your skin tone
- 5 × blouses/tops – colours that suit your skin tone as well as both black and coloured jackets
- 2 shirts – white and another colour to suit your skin tone and your coloured jacket
- 1 structured leather handbag that fits A4 folders (black)
- 1 smaller clutch that fits inside your larger handbag
- 7 pairs stockings – 4 black sheer, 3 tan
- 2 pairs court shoes – black and nude
- 1 pair structured black flat shoes (in case you have to walk a lot)
- Accessories – gold, silver, pearls – simple, classic
- Hair and makeup – simple, elegant and neat. If hair is long, wear up for a more serious, professional look

Suggested labels:

Farage	www.farage.com.au
Carla Zampatti	www.carlazampatti.com.au
Portmans	www.portmans.com.au
Cue	www.cue.cc
Veronika Maine	www.veronikamaine.com.au
Zara	www.zara.com

The basics of a professional man's wardrobe

- 2 suits (2 pairs of pants for each jacket) in charcoal grey and French Navy
- 1 lightweight blazer
- 2 pairs tailored trousers that will go with the blazer

- 3 crisp white shirts (and add variety with textured patterns in white)
- 2 French blue shirts (different shades of blue)
- 3 silk ties (the smaller and more symmetrical the pattern, the more formal, conservative and elegant the look)
- 2 pairs black leather shoes (lace-ups look more professional)
- 1 black leather belt
- Cufflinks – simple and elegant white or yellow gold cufflinks if you opt for French cuffs for some of your shirts; this is a very elegant look!
- Watch – leather or metal straps; no digital watches, please!
- Hair – well groomed, use a little product if your hair is unruly

Suggested labels:

Bluefly	www.bluefly.com
Anthony Squires	ww.anthonysquires.com.au
Zegna	www.zegna.com

What about colour?

If you asked me to dress someone in clothing that would open business doors and their twin in clothing that would have doors slammed in their face, the first distinction I'd apply is colour.

In Western cultures, the general rule is that dark colours project more authority. Imagine barristers in a pale grey or police officers in pretty pink – the wearers would lose their visual authority. In business wear for men, a dark navy or charcoal suit is a visually foolproof way of projecting seriousness and professionalism.

When it comes to choosing specific colours, keep the following in mind:

Grey

Grey projects neutrality and reliability. I love grey because it suits almost all skin tones. It's flattering and elegant.

There are hundreds of shades of grey and every one of them has a story. Some are warm, some cold, some neutral and some peculiar. Greys are stable, practical and won't let you down.

Navy

Navy conveys conservative authority. It's a good choice for a strict budget, but not always favoured by those at the top – one client called it the 'colour of middle management'. Navy downplays gender differences in business wear. My favourite is French Navy, which is the darkest navy, almost black.

Black

Black is sophisticated, bold and mysterious. It projects formality and is useful in establishing new professional boundaries.

Beige/tan/stone

These neutrals are the least threatening of business colours. Subject to styling, these shades can be boring when unrelieved by a contrasting colour; or can convey a quiet chic. (Thanks, Armani … so elegant!).

Red

Red has the longest wavelength of pure colours and attracts attention – packaged goods manufacturers and book cover designers love red. Wear it when you want to stand out (provided not everyone else is wearing it), but don't overdo it. Most women successfully limit red to a jacket only. When you want to adopt a low profile, red will not be your colour. However, for a presentation, red is exciting and generates visual interest and attention.

Colours to avoid

Pastels

Nursery or gelato shades convey less visual credibility than mid to darker shades. However, there are exceptions in very hot, tropical, climates. It all depends on what is appropriate in your geographic location. Also consider your own skin tone – light blonde hair and blue eyes work best with paler colours such a baby blue or pink; however, those colours don't convey authority.

Brights

While brights are memorable, 'good news' colours, they can compete with communication that's intended to be serious and respectful; for example, a TV journalist in hot pink covering news about a school bus disaster, or a politician in banana yellow delivering a controversial policy wouldn't appear appropriate.

Browns and greens

Some people think that brown suits are sartorial suicide or 'career-limiting'. If you ignore these comments, please wear the deepest of chocolate brown or brown/black and have it exquisitely tailored. I'd simply avoid greens unless your skin tone is beautifully enhanced by an elegant olive green tone.

General advice

As a general rule, the further you deviate from conventional greys and navies, the better the quality has to be. This includes beiges and teals and, dare I say, the deepest of browns!

The cooler the climate, the stronger the correlation between dark shades and authority. If very dark fabrics make you look funereal, a mid-blue or grey fabric with a light tie will lighten the mood.

Some of you will insist on following the latest fashion trends with unusual colours. Unless you have unlimited resources (and can't possibly wear any colour unless it belongs to this season), for corporate success stick with the classics. You can always update a look simply with an accessory in the most current shade that goes well with a classic outfit.

Body language

When you are out to impress someone, especially at an interview or during a networking meeting, once you are well prepared, have done your research and know what you are going to say, and have decided what to wear that will be appropriate for the occasion, it's time to think about how you come across with your mannerisms and your body language.

Whether you are pitching for a contract or being interviewed for a job, your body language will affect the outcome. So many of us just don't think about our own body language and yet we are so affected by the body language of others. The little clues that will indicate to the person sitting across from you if you are nervous, being genuine, or telling a story that doesn't ring true will come from not just your tone of voice, but also (mainly) from your body language.

When you meet someone, steady eye contact, a warm smile and a firm, confident handshake says, 'It's a pleasure to meet you!' When you say it, a positive, genuine tone of voice conveys authenticity.

Interviewers can read a person's body language quickly. What this means is that if you've made a positive impression, the interviewer will spend the rest of the time looking for confirmation of this positive image. Conversely, if you make a negative first impression often the interviewer will spend the rest of the time looking for more evidence that you are not right for the job.

Here are a few tips that will help you to project a positive image:
- Eye contact and good posture are the most important forms of non-verbal communication. Maintaining steady eye contact helps to create the impression of confidence and honesty. Most

of the information about you comes from your face because that's what they are looking at. Your eyes are most important, followed by your facial expressions. Be aware though, that holding someone's gaze for too long can be disconcerting.

- Your handshake is of vital importance. This is the only physical contact you will be making with your client or interviewer. A firm handshake is mandatory. This conveys confidence. How have you felt when receiving a 'limp fish' handshake? What did you think of that person?
- Your posture says a great deal about whether you care about the way you present yourself, whether you care about what you have to offer and whether you are even aware of the impression you may give. Pull yourself up to your full height, lean forward with a smile when you are shaking hands with your potential client or the interviewer. When seated don't slouch, sit slightly forward. This conveys that you want to understand exactly what is being said.
- When seated, sit with your backside right up against the back of the chair. This will ensure that you sit upright and don't slouch. This also prevents you from perching on the edge of the chair like a bird about to take flight. Whether or not you cross your legs is up to you but be aware of your foot movements – too much jiggling of your foot will make you look nervous and also be distracting to the interviewer.

Your experienced image

What is it like to be in your presence? The experience people have with you creates your experienced image, and this image can overrule all the others and cause people to think differently about you.

From that first handshake (is yours a limp fish or power handshake?), your tone of voice, your attitude to work and to life, your sense of humour, your manners, whether you are someone who looks for opportunities or only sees obstacles, whether you smile easily or scowl as the norm – all of this counts towards what it's like to be with you.

Think about the experience others have with you. Do you talk over people, do you defer to others, do you make introductions politely, do you listen to what others say, and do you seem to care? Do you do what is considered to be the right thing in various circumstances? This is particularly important when dealing with people across cultures – what is acceptable in your culture may not be acceptable in theirs.

One of my clients had the unusual habit of allowing her accent to change every time we went through interview practice sessions. She was a very senior executive with a Sydneysider Australian accent; however, every time we went through interview questions in a formal interview practice session her accent changed and she sounded extremely English and quite posh!

She denied it when I brought it up; she was totally unaware. When I recorded a session with her, she then realised what I was saying was true and immediately was able to take action on it. It was an important part of her experienced image as her anxiety during the interview process was affecting her natural communication style.

Your proven image

While first impressions count, if you create a negative first impression, you can overcome it in time. You overcome it by creating a consistent, reliable proven image.

One of my clients explained that early on in her current role she missed a few important deadlines on major projects due to conflicting personal issues she was experiencing. This frustrated her manager and her teammates, as it affected their work and they were not aware of what was going on in her personal life. Her manager gave her lesser projects to work on, and it affected her reputation at work.

In order to overcome this she had to openly communicate with her manager her circumstances so he understood her challenges and then she worked extra hard to meet expectations consistently. It took about 6 months of steady successes before her manager gained full confidence in her ability to deliver on major projects.

Creating a positive proven image means not over promising and under delivering; it means over delivering and creating a consistently positive customer or client experience.

It means taking the necessary steps to deliver on time, within budget, keep your promises and be consistent in your delivery. It means becoming the dependable mentor, the reliable employee or the manager who genuinely cares. It means building your positive reputation one step at a time.

What's most important is to be true to yourself and to be authentic in all that you do. If your hidden image, assumed image, visual image, experienced image and proven image are consistent and complement each other, and reflect your personal and career values, you will be successful, respected and perceived as someone who displays strong personal leadership characteristics.

EXPLORE JOB SEARCH STRATEGIES THAT WORK

"Nothing in the world can take the place of persistence. Talent will not; nothing is more common than unsuccessful men with talent. Genius will not; unrewarded genius is almost a proverb. Education will not; the world is full of educated derelicts.

Persistence and determination alone are omnipotent. The slogan 'press on' has solved and will always solve the problems of the human race."

— Calvin Coolidge

A little while ago, I heard a woman describing her plight on talkback radio.

She contacted the presenter on air, feeling desperate about her job search situation. Her role was made redundant at the beginning of the year and she'd been applying for about five jobs a day online for the last five months. In that time she'd only had three interviews, none of which progressed.

Amanda's fifty-five years old, holds a Bachelor of Arts degree and a Diploma of Education, has extensive experience in facilities and office management and although she was applying for similar roles, and also lesser roles, she was getting nowhere. She sounded at the end of her tether and my heart went out to her.

The presenter then asked her if she thought it was because of her age and she said that it probably was. That was when I was prompted to call the radio station to offer my assistance to her, gratis, as she needed guidance and a reality check on how to look for a job, regardless of her age.

We set up an in-depth consultation, which included a reality check, review of her resume and job search strategies. She was just grateful to have someone to point her in the right direction!

During our discussions I discovered that all she had been doing was logging on to www.seek.com.au, www.mycareer.com.au and www.careerone.com.au to apply for jobs.

As we spoke, a light bulb switched on as she realised she wasn't supposed to stay behind the computer looking at online job boards all day every day. While online job boards have their place, by focusing solely on them, she was missing out on a range of other job search strategies. In fact, there were six methods she could consider:

1. Using online job boards
2. Working with recruiters
3. Networking
4. Approaching employers directly
5. Interning
6. Volunteering

She decided to expand her job search activities to include networking and leveraging her network to gain introductions to decision makers in the companies she really wanted to work in. Within 2 months she secured a new role through one of her new network connections. I was delighted when she told me, "I thought my only way of getting a job was by applying to advertised roles.

Just one introduction to the right person set a chain of events that have led to this new job that I would never have known about otherwise!"

This chapter will show you how to take advantage of these job search strategies, so you can find your next role without the five-month wait.

1. How to use online job boards effectively

Job boards are a great way to learn about available positions that meet your requirements – their search filters are sophisticated enough that you can tailor a search to fit your exact needs, including location, salary, industry, skill requirements and more.

The most popular job boards in Australia are:

- www.seek.com.au
- www.careerone.com.au
- www.mycareer.com.au
- www.jobsjobsjobs.com.au
- www.linkedin.com.au
- www.indeed.com.au
- www.simplyhired.com.au

Indeed and Simply Hired filter all the job boards online, making them a one-stop shop.

- www.applydirect.com.au

This job board only features roles advertised by companies who are hiring, meaning there are no recruitment agency ads.

Some large international job boards, which may include Australian jobs, are:

- www.monster.com (predominantly US jobs)
- www.jobsdb.com (key focus on jobs in Asia)
- www.efinancialcareers.com

So many of my clients tell me that they have done 'everything' to look for a job and 'nothing' is happening. Some have felt quite despondent and just can't figure out what to do to change things.

What I always say is, "If something isn't working, do something different." More often than not, 'everything' has been sitting on the internet, looking on job boards, and making applications by clicking on the 'Apply' button, sending the same resume over and over again. Does this sound familiar?

Of course this method *can* work and many have found their new roles through internet applications; however, it is not the most effective way to use these job boards. Let's consider what a job board could tell you.

First of all, most recruitment agencies use online job boards to post job advertisements to find suitable candidates for roles they are currently working on. That means when you scan through the job descriptions on each job board you will see which recruitment agencies are very active in a specific industry or job function. That's valuable information, as it will give you an idea as to which recruitment agencies would probably be interested in your skill sets or industry knowledge.

Second, you may notice that a company is advertising directly for several roles in different departments, or several roles of a similar capacity. What that tells you is that there is growth within that company. Therefore, even if the roles advertised are not exactly what you are looking for, if the company is expanding, perhaps it's worthwhile making a direct approach to a potential hiring manager or decision maker to explore future options.

Third, as you look through various job advertisements you may notice that a certain industry seems to be particularly active and other industries are not advertising or hiring. Consider industry trends when job seeking. It makes sense to be aware of industries where there is growth rather than a hiring freeze across the board.

A few years ago I conducted several career workshops at a major investment bank in Sydney where the plan was a massive reduction in headcount over the course of the next 12 months. At that time there were few advertised roles in the financial services sector as other organisations in this sector had imposed a hiring freeze.

Of course there were few roles for those job seekers looking for another role in the financial services sector. All of those looking for the same or similar job in the same industry were in for an extremely challenging job search. To open up new opportunities they needed to leverage their transferrable skills to see where they would fit in a different industry.

Fourth, the advertisements on the job boards give you information about the recruitment agency, the company advertising and, if you're lucky, the name and contact information of the person hiring so you can call or email for more details.

What all this tells us is that online job boards are great for research as well as to find and apply for specific job openings.

Once you've reviewed the job advertisement, taking the above research ideas into consideration, then what do you do if you decide that you want to apply?

I'm always amazed at the number of clients who tell me that they find a job online, attach their resume, click Apply and then are disappointed if they don't get a response at all, let alone a screening interview. What we expect to happen is that all applications get read and screened, and all applicants receive a 'thanks for your application' email or at least a 'no thanks' email.

In reality, it would help if you took a bit more action before clicking on the apply button.

How to apply for advertised roles

1. Print the advertisement and highlight the key attributes that are essential to be considered for the role, and also the additional preferences that they are looking for. Have you got those skills? If so, are they reflected in the professional profile section of your resume and also identified in the professional history section?
2. Check and see if there is a contact person and their details included in the job ad. If so, pick up the phone and call them! If you reach the contact person, let them know that you are interested in the role and that you'd like to be sure you will be a contender. Give them your Introductory Pitch (tailored for this specific role). Ask if they are able to provide more information. You could be lucky and gain additional background information that will help you to tailor your cover letter and resume so that your relevant experience and skills are in a more prominent position in your resume.
3. Ask if they would like you to go through the online process for the submission or if they would like you to email your resume directly. (When I was in recruitment I was always impressed if a potential candidate took the initiative this way as it demonstrated that they really were keen on the role.) Many people just submit applications during their lunch break without much thought and it shows.
4. Armed with this additional information, tailor your resume and cover letter. Many online applications are screened by an Applicant Tracking System (ATS) which

parses your documents looking for key word matches to what is in the job description. Ensure the relevant key words for the skills you possess are covered. Then, make your application. If the screener agreed that you could email them directly, make sure that in the subject heading of the email you include your name again, the reference number of the job advertisement and also the job title. Make it easy for your name to be remembered.

5. If you receive an automated response, then you know you are in the system. If you don't, call to check that your application has been received. There are occasional system errors.

6. If you receive a screening call, terrific! If you don't receive any word after a week or so, call to follow up. Many clients feel uncomfortable calling to follow up and don't want to 'bother' the screener in case. To be honest, what have you got to lose by following up? Either the screener takes your call or he or she doesn't take your call. If your call is taken, it means you've got another chance to potentially sell yourself. Say that you are following up to find out if you are in consideration for the role. If you're told you are, then wait for the next step. If you're told you're not then you can move on – there will be other roles on which you can spend your time more profitably.

So that's it. Have you been doing all of these things? If not, it's worth a go, as it will increase the chances of your resume being read.

As I mentioned earlier, I wrote and published an article on LinkedIn entitled, 'Do You Appear Desperate by Following Up?' Within one week, it generated 49,000 views, over 1,700 shares and over 200 comments – that's a great deal of debate as to whether or not to follow up. There is obviously a lot of anxiety about making the call or the follow-up email. What I suggest always is, if you haven't heard back and it's causing you anxiety or frustration, make contact. It's good to know one way or another to put your mind at rest or to let go and focus on other opportunities.

2. Working with recruitment consultants

Ah, now it's time to discuss recruiters. Whenever a client discussion turns to recruitment consultants, there is usually a lot of complaining along the lines of, "They never return phone calls", "I apply and then I hear nothing", "They never follow up to let me know what's happening in the process". And the complaining goes on.

There are incredibly professional and consultative recruitment consultants who DO return phone calls, who always let their candidates know how they're going in the process and who keep you in the loop at all times. Unfortunately, there are others who don't. As my client, the Financial Controller, discovered, "It was hard working with some recruiters who would not return phone calls or provide any feedback on why I didn't get a role. Some of those recruiters were very friendly when I was working and needed to hire more staff, but when the shoe was on the other foot and I needed their assistance, I found them quite disinterested."

Why is this so?

The recruitment process

Recruiters work for their customer, first and foremost. The customer is not you, the candidate; their customer is whoever pays the recruitment cost – typically the company looking to hire. The customer outsources the recruitment process because they don't have the time or resources to conduct an effective search themselves. Therefore a recruitment consultant MUST do a good job screening candidates and will only put forward those who are most likely to be successful in the role that is being advertised.

This means the process starts long before a role is advertised – recruiters typically consult with their customer to gain a detailed understanding of their requirements, including the key areas of expertise they require, the organisational structure, the role's responsibilities and the ideal candidate background, as well as understanding behavioural competency requirements and technical skills needed for the positions.

Most recruiters initially source suitable candidates via their database, via LinkedIn and via their grapevine. If there aren't enough suitable candidates that they can approach, then they will advertise. If they advertise, then you go through the application process mentioned in the previous section.

The recruiter will screen resumes for the candidates who have the right skills, the right amount of experience, the relevant industry experience and previous experience in that job function. That means that the closer you match all of the requirements, the greater the likelihood that you will be called in for an interview. That is, IF your resume is read! (Take note of the application process mentioned under *How to use online job boards effectively* and return to *Resumes and marketing materials* for more information on getting your resume up to scratch.)

Once resumes have been screened, a recruitment agent will then conduct preliminary interviews before shortlisting candidates for an interview with their customer.

The interview process can vary somewhat depending on the recruiter. Rachel Rodwell, Partner of Prime Axis, an international and domestic executive search and recruitment service for the wealth management industry, describes Prime Axis's process:

"As a search business, our clients expect extensive profiling as opposed to a summary introduction. Therefore, as a minimum, screening normally consists of a 30-minute telephone assessment focusing on functional and technical skill compatibility then a 1-hour face-to-face meeting assessing personal attributes and cultural alignment followed by an in-depth discussion addressing the key competencies of the role (approximately an hour to an hour-and-a-half)."

Evolve People, a specialist boutique recruitment consultancy for the Procurement & Supply Chain profession across Australasia, "interview all [their] candidates by telephone or face to face, and assess not only their behavioural competencies but also their technical skill set. [They] use flexible means for each requirement and if the client needs something specific, [they] can design specific questioning for the role(s) and design and provide a scorecard of responses to help them to understand the reasoning behind [their] selection process."

Brad Eisenhouth, Former Director of Absolute Executive Recruitment (AXR), a specialist finance recruitment firm focusing on the commercial and industrial sector, focuses on assessing whether a candidate is able to deliver against the challenges of the job they are looking to fill. "We need to find out their strengths and what may make them unique to our client. For example, if we needed someone who could implement a shared service function in a large, complex business, we'd look at examples of their successes and how they influence people to get on board, what systems or best practices they used during the process in terms of implementing projects and what they would do differently to be even more successful. This would give us an idea of their ability to implement solutions."

After the initial interviews, the recruitment agent will provide their customer with a shortlist of recommended candidates.

Throughout the process, communication is crucial – both with the business hiring, and with you, the candidate. As Rachel says, "A business invests in a search consultant on critical roles which invariably have high visibility in the business – the pressure is on! So much can change in a search – a business may restructure, the market may not support the desires of the client, priorities of the role may change during the process. Each of these things impacts the candidates and process significantly. If you are not partnering and communicating with your client regularly, you and the candidates could get caught short, which means longer lead times and mismanaged expectations."

Once the customer has further cut the shortlist, the recruitment agent will then check the candidate's referees to help the customer make a final decision.

Working with recruiters on a career change

If recruiters are looking for candidates who already have the right skills, the right amount of experience, the relevant industry experience and previous experience in that job function, does that mean recruiters won't work with candidates who are seeking a career change? Not necessarily.

According to Rachel, recruiters are willing to work with candidates looking for a career change, "on the proviso the transferable skills are present and the candidate is realistic about the journey ahead".

So what are these transferrable skills? According to Rachel, "self-awareness is a key skill for candidates looking to make a career change, in addition to tenacity and resilience."

However, she continues that, "As an industry professional, I am happy to draw out the information required to assess compatibility to a role and what those key transferable skills are; however, not everyone is prepared to do that. One of the impacts of the global financial crisis is that employers have been and, to an extent, still are more comfortable to recruit 'like for like'. They have not had to think out of the box and it is important to not assume they will recognise those transferable skills. Candidates looking for a career change have to work harder to communicate why they should be considered for a role over someone who already has the desired industry experience. I need to know a candidate can think on their feet and articulate that to a client."

Likewise, Jenny Wong and Odelle Brown, Former Executive Directors of Evolve People, say they have successfully found work for candidates with a non-procurement background in procurement or supply.

However, like Rachel, they advise that a candidate needs certain qualities to make this work. "This can only happen if the client is open-minded and flexible with their approach to the technical procurement skills requirements, and if the interpersonal skills are more important. We have seen cases like this when we are recruiting for a procurement role and the client insists on a subject matter expert, such as a Category Manager for Marketing or IT&T. Candidates who have come from a Marketing or IT department can successfully transfer their career into a Procurement department."

If you struggle to find a recruiter who can help with a career change, then you can leverage your network rather than going through a recruiter. (More on this later in the networking section of this chapter.) A recruiter's role is to place the most suitable candidate in a role for their customer, and the candidate considered most likely to hit the ground running and succeed will be one who has done the same job, or a similar job in the same or a similar industry within a company of a similar size and culture.

Reaching out to recruiters

What about approaching recruiters so that they get to know you even if they don't have a suitable role at this point in time? I suggest that you do your research – check to see which consultancy is active in the types of roles you are seeking within the industry sectors you are considering. If there is a consultant's name that pops up regularly for certain roles, then that consultant will be a good one to contact for an exploratory conversation.

Jenny and Odelle recommend candidates contact recruiters by phone and email. "Phone is the best way as, if you get through to the consultant, then you can provide a brief introduction about yourself and try to arrange a meeting with them to register."

Brad is happy for candidates to contact his firm directly but, "You must make a good case for us to meet with you. If you have a strong introduction via email or a phone call, a compelling value proposition, clarity with regard to what you are looking for and if you are relevant for the types of roles we fill, then of course we will be happy to meet with you."

If you are fortunate enough to get through to the consultant, be sure to have your introductory pitch ready so that you can explain who you are, what you do and what you are looking for. Ask them if they specialise in your area and, if so, tell them that you'd like to meet them so that you both can get to know each other for future roles if he or she is not currently working on something suitable.

However there are times when the direct approach will not work. Top recruiters explain, "The best way for a candidate to get noticed by us is to be recommended or introduced directly by someone who has worked with us before. We match the right skills with the right business, the team culture and the environment. There are many factors to consider when finding the ideal candidate. We're looking at the top 10% of applicants in their respective fields."

Consultants seek to secure quality candidates in their database. Make yourself valuable to them. Help them to be interested in you and want to meet you by being well prepared with your approach and your responses.

Once you've met with the recruiter, you'll know if there is synergy and if they are interested in keeping in touch. Ask if they'd be happy to connect with you on LinkedIn. (That's always a good thing to do as it gives you the opportunity to stay on the recruiter's radar through your regular LinkedIn activity updates, plus it's easier to turn up in a key word search on LinkedIn if you are a primary connection.)

Ask if it would be okay to touch base with them every three to four weeks to see how the market is going. After the meeting, don't forget to send them a thank you email for their time and reinforce what you have to offer by mentioning the key points that captured their attention during your meeting. Then keep your fingers crossed and find the next person to network with!

How to be a great candidate

Being a great candidate is more than simply having the technical skills and experience that a position requires.

According to Jenny and Odelle, the ideal candidate "will display and have demonstrated personal qualities such as effective communication skills, negotiation skills, stakeholder engagement and influencing skills, commercial acumen, integrity and listening skills".

They consider the technical skills to be a prerequisite, while interpersonal skills, especially "the ability to engage and influence stakeholders", are what make the difference.

Likewise, Rachel looks for self-awareness, commercial acumen, motivation, initiative and the ability to engage at every level. She also emphasises the importance of communication: "This may seem basic but I cannot stress how critical this is – the ability to adapt a communication style to the audience, recognise what is being asked/required and structure accordingly."

However, communication needs to be demonstrated, particularly in your relationship with the recruiter. Rachel advises candidates to "demonstrate initiative, confidence and follow up. I'm happy for a candidate to call, email or send me a note on LinkedIn – just reach out!"

Brad reinforces, "If you haven't heard back from the recruiter after an interview, wait until after the time frame you've been advised before making contact to find out if you are still in contention. There is usually plenty on their plate and it is in their interest to successfully fill the job. Making contact is important, especially if you have received another offer and need to make a decision. Sharing developments in your situation is a much more effective way of managing the relationship than simply calling for an update."

When it comes to getting noticed by a recruiter, Rachel advises candidates:

"Call, follow up with a resume and then another call. Recruiters don't have the best reputation in being responsive; however, this is often because they tend to be incredibly stretched. Don't be put off and wait for the call. As frustrating as it may be, be tenacious. Ultimately it is up to the candidate to manage their career searches."

Final advice from the recruiters

On a final note, when I was speaking to these recruiters, I asked if they had any specific advice for job seekers.

Rachel said, "Give yourself time to really think through your skill set and what you want. Know your market; be informed and proactive in your approach. It is all about activity. This is very attractive to any recruiter and future employer; it says to them you are not waiting for the role to come to you and these qualities are likely to be reflected in how you perform in a role.

"Don't succumb to the pressure to secure a role as quickly as possible; make sure your resume reflects who you are and that you are prepared for hard questions. In my 17 years of recruitment, the candidates I see who rush these first, basic but critical, steps often end up retracing them and missing out on initial opportunities because the client has deselected these candidates as they are not clear on where they sit in the business."

Odelle and Jenny advise clients: "Prepare an effective resume – this is your strategic document and a first impression to a Recruitment Consultant and a Hiring Manager. Use multiple sourcing strategies to find vacancies e.g. job websites, specialist recruitment firms, company websites, and networks. Be realistic about your skills and knowledge and, therefore, the roles you apply for. Have a positive attitude when going through the process of job searching and be persistent; the ideal role may come around when you least expect it!" and they all sum it up with, "It's a numbers game. Find ways to keep yourself motivated and stay fresh in the process."

If you'd like more information on either using online job boards or how to work with recruitment consultants, follow me on Instagram www.instagram.com/janecareercoach for regular updates on tips and techniques in the job search process.

And for on-going support find many free resources at www.thecareersacademy.online

3. Networking

Whenever I've conducted career transition workshops, or discussed networking with clients, I've always found some people are reluctant to give networking a try because they have a picture in their mind of some smooth talker coming up to them, shoving a business card in their hand and saying, "Call me".

I get it – if anyone does that to me, I cringe!

This isn't what I mean by 'networking'. To me, networking is simply building relationships with people so you can share information and contacts to help each other, whether professionally or socially.

If you think about it this way, you're probably already networking – if you've ever asked a friend to recommend a product or a service that would best suit your requirements (a good hairdresser, physiotherapist or advice on the benefits of the car you've been considering), you've used your network to gather information for your own benefit. (I just hope the recommendations were good ones!)

We've already gone through the most commonly used methods to look for a job. Now let's talk about the most *effective* method.

According to a survey by Right Management, part of global staffing giant Manpower Group, networking is the best way to find a new role. The survey analysed data from 59,133 candidates they advised over a three-year period, and found 41% landed a job through networking.

Source of New Job	2010
Networking	41%
Internet Job Board	25%
Agency/Search Firm	11%
Direct Approach	8%
Online Network (2010)	4%
Advertisement	2%
Other	10%

Carly McVey, Right Management's former Vice President of Career Management, commented on the rapidly blurring lines between traditional and online networking. Said McVey in the release from Right Management: "Online social networking may not always be separate from traditional networking since one so often leads to the other. A job seeker uses the internet to track down former associates or acquaintances and then reaches out to them in person." The numbers haven't changed too much since 2010, as the 2014 Jobvite Hiring Report revealed that a personal connection and recommendation resulted in 40% of job seekers securing their next role.

And what do job seekers say? My clients have commented:

"I was amazed at the opportunities that came to light over a $3 coffee! I'd recommend spending a solid two or three days a week dedicated to this because I realised that finding a job was my new job for a while."

"I learned that the key to success was networking, networking, networking ... Some people talk about serendipity and I found that you can create your own serendipity by turning up and meeting people who are experts in the areas you are exploring."

"My extensive networking activities always provided me with new opportunities and the more people I spoke to, the more opportunities presented themselves. Every morning I'd look at my list of contacts and pick up the phone to set appointments. I found it was like a snowball; the connections just grew and grew."

So what's stopping you from networking?

When it comes to networking for professional purposes, most of us fear rejection. "What if I'm disturbing that person?" we think or, "What if they don't want to help me out?"

If worst comes to worst and you are disturbing them, they'll probably just let you know that it's not convenient to talk at that moment, so you can ask when would be a better time to speak with them and book in a time. If they don't want to or can't help you out, is it the worst thing in the world? You just thank them for taking your call, responding to your email or speaking with you and move on to your next contact.

When looking for a job, remember: You are now in sales. It's time to consider yourself as a product that needs to go to market. As with all product marketing, you need to understand the key functions and benefits of the product, conduct market research to find the customers who need those functions or benefits, the customer business needs and how you, The Product, can fill those needs. Once you are in front of the right people, the conversation begins. However, like all sales, you'll have a number of hoops to jump through before a sale is made.

In any sale, these hoops include: making initial contact (while the customer is obtaining information about the vendor or product); first contact with the sales rep (by phone or email); first face-to-face meeting with the rep; additional meetings with the rep; the formal presentation or proposal; and, finally, the vendor selection meeting.

According to the Forum Corporation Research team (www.forum.com), a buying decision is much more likely in the later stages of the sales process than in the early stages, with customers estimating their likelihood of buying at the proposal stage about twice as great as at first contact (66% versus 34%).

So what does this research mean for you? It means that you must approach networking as just the first step of your sales process. And that first step must be taken in order to create and then develop the relationship.

Step 1 – Touch points and your verbal pitch

The first step is what we consider to be a touch point. A touch point is any interaction or encounter that can influence the customer's perception of your product, service, or brand. A touch point can be intentional (an email you send out) or unintentional (someone coming across your excellent LinkedIn profile).

Your touch points include every encounter in the attraction process, such as your LinkedIn profile, resume, cover letter, approach emails, thank you emails, attendance at industry events, recommendations from those who know you and confirmation of your abilities by your referees.

Touch points begin long before the customer actually makes a purchase (offers you a role) and long after they have made their first transaction. (After starting the job, do you reliably deliver what you have sold?) Your goal is to create a positive and consistent experience at each touch point.

When it comes to networking, the key here is to be comfortable with what you will say when you approach a potential contact so you present a positive first impression. This is where you use your verbal pitch, as discussed in *Resumes and your marketing communication.*

You will adjust this pitch depending on the person you are approaching – it will be more casual if it's a friend or close colleague, and more structured if it's someone to whom you've been introduced through your close connections.

Step 2 – Your networking list

Once you know what you will say when making a networking approach to different audiences, it's time to make a list of contacts who could assist you in the exploration and information-gathering part of your marketing campaign. This list will also keep you on track and accountable to take timely action.

	Friends/ Family	General Network	Target Network	Company Name	Contact Date	Outcome	Follow-Up Date
1							
2							
3							
4							
5							
6							
7							
8							
9							
10							

Keep growing this list throughout your marketing campaign.

Step 3 – Feedback from friends (the PAL process)

Let's make the networking process easy for you by approaching those people who you know, like, respect and feel most comfortable with first. Essentially, you're going to get used to speaking about yourself and asking the right questions in a low-pressure situation. Let's also use this opportunity to gain some valuable feedback on how others perceive you and what others consider to be your key strengths and areas for improvement.

There's nothing like honest feedback to help us become better versions of ourselves. This is why we must respect the opinions of those we contact in this early stage. If we don't respect their opinions, then we are simply wasting time.

So how can you organise this?

1. Make an appointment to speak with friends and family members whom you respect and feel comfortable speaking with about your career.
2. Follow my **PAL** method when having your discussion with your friends (because you're comfortable with your pals!)

> Position – Ask – Listen:
>
> P – Give them your pitch, or where you are right now.
>
> A – Ask for feedback on how you are perceived, what's good, what's an area for improvement.
>
> L – Listen to their responses, take them into consideration and choose the ones on which you will take action.

3. Thank them for their time and keep them in the loop with your progress.

Taking note of the feedback you have received, use this information to 'sharpen your axe' and prepare for the next stage. You will find that the more questions you ask and feedback you gain, the more comfortable you will be with the process. You will find that you become quite used to saying your positioning statement or pitch out loud. You will naturally refine it until it flows off your tongue comfortably!

Step 4 – Networking with your general contacts (the PEARL process)

Now you have warmed up, let's take it to the next level by contacting other friends in a professional capacity – colleagues, ex-colleagues, and mentors with whom you feel comfortable having a career discussion.

Make a list of people in your general network who may be able to point you towards your list of target companies. An easy way to do this is to look up the companies on your target list on LinkedIn.

Those company pages will show you how you are connected to that company, either through someone you know who works there, or through a second connection (meaning you know someone who knows someone who works there). Put those people on your general networking list of contacts.

Another way to grow your general networking list is to consider where your close ex-colleagues are employed now. (Again, check on LinkedIn.) If they are in an area that is of interest to you, add them to your list!

The aim is to make a list of people who may be willing to assist you in your exploration and steer you closer towards your target audience.

You are taking a strategic approach to the networking process, as you want to achieve a specific outcome from each meeting.

1. Approach your general network and make an appointment for a face-to-face meeting if possible, such as a coffee catch-up or a lunch. I find that coffee is easier to set up than lunch or dinner and, if that's too hard, a telephone or Skype catch-up could work well too. Let your contact know that you'll only take up 15-20 minutes of their time. (You'll have to make sure you stick to that time so as not to take advantage. If your contact is happy to continue the discussions for longer, then that's their call.)
2. Follow the PEARL method when having this meeting (as you'll be gaining pearls of wisdom from your connections!)

> **Position – Explain – Ask – Request – Link:**
>
> **P** – Give your positioning statement, your pitch, or where you are right now.
>
> **E** – Explain your dream job and your desire to explore.
>
> **A** – Ask questions and gain feedback by asking about their industry expertise, their thoughts on the market, what they know about the industries and companies on your target list. Be open, share willingly, and ask for advice and guidance as to how they might approach the exploration process.
>
> **R** – Request referrals if they know anyone from your companies of choice who might be willing to have an exploratory conversation with you. If, by chance, they happen to know the potential decision maker in your area of interest, that will be your most valuable referral!
>
> **L** – Link them to a benefit, too. As they have given freely of their time, give something back – it could be an interesting article you email through as a thank you, some information that will benefit their business or personal interests. Of course, you will be paying for the coffee or lunch!

4. Thank them for their time and keep them in the loop if you have gained referrals.

Take note of all the insights you have gained from the conversation, make sure you send a follow-up thank you email with any additional information that may benefit your contact, and keep him or her in the loop when you make contact with the referrals.

Aim for at least three networking meetings a week. (Some coaches recommend five to ten; however, I know that if I set you easy targets to start off with, you will achieve them. Once you get in the swing of the networking process, you'll enjoy it so much that the appointments will start to flow!)

Step 5 – Meeting with a potential decision maker (the PEAK process)

Now this is the exciting bit! If you have been referred to someone who may be a decision maker at your target company, it's time to make a calculated approach.

First of all, be sure to ask your general contact if you can mention their name when you make contact with this person, or, even better, if they could facilitate the introduction. They may pick up the phone to make the connection, they may send an email, or they may make an introduction via LinkedIn. If that happens, you will be well on your way to setting up a productive meeting. If they prefer that you just mention their name when making contact, then at least you will be making a warm approach rather than a cold one. Few people enjoy making cold calls unless they really enjoy the sales process.

To prepare yourself well, make sure you do your research on the industry, the company and also a little bit about the individual you wish to speak with. Again, use Google, use LinkedIn and you may also gain some valuable information via www.glassdoor.com, which features company reviews from former and current employees.

When it comes to meeting the potential decision maker:

1. Approach them with confidence (remember, you have been referred by a mutual contact) to set up a face-to-face meeting. Provide this contact with several options for the timing of this meeting and do your best to fit in with their schedule. Many executives have very tight schedules and may also have travel plans for work, so be open to their suggestions. You could also suggest liaising with their assistant to set up a convenient time for a meeting, if that is appropriate.
2. At the networking meeting, use the **PEAK** method (as you're getting up there and closer to your goal).

Position – Explore – Align – Keep in touch:

P – Give your best pitch.

E – Explore what's happening in the industry, the challenges your contact may be experiencing, and share some relevant knowledge.

A – Align your experiences to his or her challenges – use your relevant achievements and recount your stories that link you to his or her pain points.

K – Keep in touch. Suggest a reason to maintain contact or follow up with some relevant and valuable information. (Connect on LinkedIn and request permission to follow up periodically so that you remain top of mind should an opportunity arise in the future.)

Remember, this meeting is simply an exploration and an opportunity for you to demonstrate your potential value to the organisation. You are sowing the seeds of success.

3. Thank them for their time, be open, friendly, and use positive body language regardless of the outcome of the meeting. Be sure to follow up as promised to show your interest and reliability.

And so the process goes. This is an ongoing exercise, so keep it up every week and you will find that once you open your eyes, ears and, most importantly, your mind to networking, new ideas, new opportunities and new directions will start to pop up. The key is to maintain momentum.

If things seem to stall, take stock of your process, what has worked and what hasn't and analyse each situation. If you need to tweak your process a bit, do so and monitor your progress. Treat this as a fascinating exploration into how far the networking process will take you.

I love to recommend that my clients 'dance in the moment'. Remain curious, remain open and the opportunities will come.

4. Approaching employers directly

From the statistics at the beginning of the networking section, you now know that a very small number of candidates found employment through directly approaching employers.

However, while it's successful for a small percentage only, it is a method that is still working for some people, and it has worked for some of my clients. So it would be foolish not to give it a try.

It's possible to enhance a direct approach by combining it with effective networking to gather more information and potentially gain a referral. Once you gain a referral, you won't be making a 'cold call' approach.

How can you do this? Focus on expanding your network to include people at your company of choice. Use LinkedIn and Facebook to find friends and contacts who are connected to that company, then reach out to those contacts through personalised emails and phone calls. This turns your direct approach into a networking process that has, statistically, been proven to be more effective.

Now, if all else fails, then you will have to make that cold, direct approach. However, nothing ventured, nothing gained! If, despite all efforts, you cannot gain a referral into the company of your dreams, find out who the decision maker is in your target department and send a well-crafted email highlighting your value in their area, along with your tailored resume. Ensure that your highlighted achievements are those that will generate a 'Wow!' from the reader.

Think of this email as a cover letter, and use the sample cover letter in *Resumes and marketing materials* to help you.

At the end of your cover letter, be positive. Try something along the lines of:

"Please find attached my resume for your interest. I understand there may not be a position available for someone with my skills and experience at this point in time; however, I would welcome the opportunity to have an exploratory conversation with you about my relevant capabilities. I will make contact within the week to set up a mutually convenient time to speak."

Tailor this to suit your personality and make sure that you call this contact within the week. If you can't get through and you are only able to reach his/her assistant, let them know that you have made contact with the decision maker in the past week and this is a follow-up call to set a time to meet.

You need to be brave; however, it's worth the effort if you really want to get in front of a decision maker in your dream company. The choice is yours.

5. Internships

"I'm too old to intern!" I can hear you say. Most people think that interning is for high school or university students. Not necessarily. In fact, it's an option for anyone who wants to gain some experience in a new area where they need to find out what it's really like in that environment, or anyone who would like to gain some initial experience before deciding if this is the right direction. Obviously it's not usual for older job seekers to intern, but where there is a will there will always be an opportunity if you approach it in the right way.

Jennifer's Story

Jennifer holds a Bachelor's Degree in Communication and possesses an incredible passion for fashion. She had successfully worked her way to a Showroom Manager role at a boutique fashion public relations agency in Sydney and was determined to move to London to further her career.

At the age of 25, Jennifer decided to make a change in direction and move from Sydney to London without any career support network. Her target was to work, client side, for a global fashion company, but she didn't know anyone in that company and she was aware that, globally, the company receives thousands of applications per week from fashionistas who would do anything to work there. She realised that she needed to develop her network in London, so she tapped into the knowledge of her friends, made lots of phone calls and managed to secure an internship at a well-known fashion magazine. This was unpaid, expenses covered only.

The network she developed through interning led to a number of interviews at other companies and then a foot in the door to her dream company! After a vigorous interview process she secured an entry-level role and now, three years later, she has been promoted three times and thriving in her chosen environment. The internship in the right industry helped her to grow her network so she could nab her dream job.

This may not be for everyone; however, it is an option to consider.

To land an internship you will have to first identify the decision maker at all the companies on your target list.

Then, treat it as if you are going through the normal job search process. However, let it be known that you are offering your services to gain experience in a specific area in an unpaid (or expenses-only) capacity. Be aware, though, that you will most likely be expected to pitch in and be hands on wherever needed. The main benefit is that you will have the chance to expand your connections in your company or industry of choice.

As mentioned in the section *Approaching Employers Directly*, find out who the decision maker is in the desired department of your target company and send a well-crafted email highlighting your value in their area, and attach your resume. Ensure that your highlighted achievements are those that are relevant to the type of role you are hoping to gain experience in.

Use the sample cover letter in *Resumes and marketing materials* to help you.

At the end of your cover letter you can add something along these lines:

"Please find attached my resume. I would welcome the opportunity to have an exploratory conversation about a possible internship in your company. I will make contact within the week to set up a mutually convenient time to speak."

For official professional internship programmes, as a rule of thumb they are offered to those currently studying in a specific field or have graduated within the last 24 months. Usually they are for those who are aged 18-30 and the programmes vary between 6 and 26 weeks in duration. If you want to find out more you can research information from many intern information websites including:

- www.internoptions.com
- www.internships.com.au
- www.navitas-careers-and-internships.com

6. Volunteering

Similarly to taking an internship, volunteering your services can be even more rewarding if it's benefiting a not-for-profit (NFP) organisation. You will have the chance to learn new skills and systems, discover a new industry and make some new friends, as well as contribute to a cause.

Donating your time to a charitable organisation provides you with a sense of satisfaction, knowing that you are helping those less fortunate than yourself. If you are really struggling with the job search, and you are losing your sense of self, volunteering can put a wonderful perspective back to your life. Knowing that you have a responsibility to turn up and provide a service on certain days helps you to stay focused and gives you a reason to get up in the mornings.

In addition to feeding your soul, volunteering also puts you in front of others who are open and willing to donate their time for others. Many who do so are also working elsewhere, and this could give you an opportunity to develop new contacts. Remember, the more people you meet, the more you open yourself up to new opportunities and ideas.

This may even lead you to discover that you wish to work full time in the NFP sector! Those who are targeting this sector would be wise to donate their time in the early days of transitioning, as it demonstrates that you genuinely want to help others.

Jo Green, one of my clients who made a career change from the corporate sector to the not-for-profit sector, is now the Fundraising Campaign Co-ordinator at Caritas.

"Moving into the non-for-profit sector can be tricky due to the change in focus, salary level, resources available such as budget for marketing, IT, HR, and so on, but it is a rewarding area to work in. The people you work with tend to be passionate and friendly, but quite often there is more work than people, which can mean taking on things that you might not quite have expected!"

When transitioning into the NFP sector, Jo started at Clean Up Australia, then worked in Community Fundraising at CanTeen before taking on her role at Caritas.

Jo recommends, "Work out the types of NFPs you are interested in (health, education, environment, animals, etc.) This will help you narrow your search field and is a question recruitment consultants always ask.

"NFPs always ask for experience in the sector when you apply for a role. I was lucky that I got my foot in the door of a NFP by initially securing a six-month contract, but I would advise people to get some volunteer experience on their resume, even if just for a few hours, to show where their passion lives and that this is an important part of their life."

Opportunities for volunteers in the NFP sector can be found at numerous charities, along with general sites like www.probono australia.com.au in Australia, which lists non-profit organisations supporting aged care, children, animals, cancer support, education, health, research, youth programmes, homelessness, libraries – the list is extensive.

A great resource for global non-profits is www.topnonprofits.com, which lists both lesser-known and well-known organisations, including UNICEF, Oxfam, Rotary, Lions Club, Samaritans, World Wildlife Fund, TED Talks and World Vision. Again, the list of great organisations is extensive so you can choose your strongest area of interest to explore.

Whether it is fundraising, coordinating events, providing accounting services, or helping those in need, there are always opportunities for volunteers. If this is financially viable for you, even if only for a few months, it may reward you in more ways than you expect.

RELATE YOUR SUITABILITY AT INTERVIEWS

"One important key to success is self-confidence. An important key to self-confidence is preparation."

– Arthur Ashe

With your marketing materials and professional image up to scratch, and your job search strategies running at full throttle, you will start getting interviews.

Over my years as a career coach and also during my time as a recruiter, I've interviewed and conducted practice interviews with hundreds of candidates and clients. I've found that there's always an element of anxiety surrounding interviews and I'm often asked questions like "What do I say when they ask …", "What do they really want when they say …" and "Why would they ask *that*?"

I like to think of an interview as a conversation with an agenda. The conversation may be formal and structured or casual and friendly, but there will always be an agenda, both for the interviewer and the interviewee.

In a larger company, a good resume might generate an initial phone-screening interview. The hiring manager will have provided the screener with specific requirements for the role. Note: We hope that those requirements don't change during the selection process

– sometimes changes do happen. This can be frustrating for the screener and the recruiter, and disappointing to the applicant.

Following the phone-screening interview, if you are granted a face-to-face interview, there are several hoops to jump through, including interviews, feedback, more questions, and more interviews. These interviews might be one-on-one or panel interviews; there may be psychometric assessments, skills assessments and/or role-play situations, and presentations to be made as part of the selection process. Between each stage there will be a waiting period, often agonising for the candidate. If the process continues successfully there will be reference checks, salary negotiations, background checks and finally – hopefully – an offer.

By contrast, if it's a very small company without set HR policies, you may find that the interview is a casual conversation to get to know you and the process is quite simple. It could end up being simply a matter of chemistry, attitude and a willingness to learn that will get you across the line.

Regardless of the type of interview, preparation is key.

Interview preparation

How much time do you spend preparing for that all-important interview? If it's 10 minutes looking at the company website to get a quick overview of what they do and then turning up and hoping that you'll be able to wing it, then I'm sorry to say that is not enough!

According to the Executive Recruiter Index released by Korn/Ferry International in 2003, which surveyed over 300 professional recruitment consultants, interviewees make four common mistakes during interviews:

The most common mistakes made during interviews	Percentage of responses
Talking too much	43%
Lack of preparation	33%
Over-inflated ego	24%
Bad hygiene/inappropriate attire	<1%

Of these mistakes, even though the most common mistake was talking too much, 41% of respondents agreed that a **lack of preparation** was the **most fatal** to a candidate's chances of securing the role.

Thus, the key to success is to prepare, prepare, prepare! Give yourself the best possible chance for success by knowing what you need to do, maintaining humility with confidence, listening to the questions and responding appropriately, and dressing for the occasion and environment.

How to prepare for your interview

Keep the following in mind in the lead-up to your interview:

1. Do your research

Research the company and industry

Do this by talking to people who already work, or have worked, in the company. (Refer to the Networking section of *Explore new job- search strategies.*)

Find out about the company, the projected directions, their corporate values and initiative and read up on news reports that could also give you an additional insight into the culture of the organisation.

Also have a look on the company website, on competitor websites, do a company search on LinkedIn and have a look at www.glassdoor.com, where you will find employee reviews, industry information and salary surveys. This is very helpful if you don't know someone or are not able to be referred to someone already working at the company.

Another good research site is www.avention.com, which has a global business browser. For a subscription you can gain company insights, industry reports, the latest news articles and reports about any company from global news sources. They offer a free, time-limited trial; however, some local libraries offer you access if you join the library. This is the most cost-effective way to access the information.

Research the job function

Using your networking strategies for referrals, look for people who have held the same job function to find out the key qualities that made them a success (or what didn't work for them).

Research the interviewer

This is especially important if you are meeting your hiring manager. If you find out something positive that you are able to bring up during the interview, this will demonstrate you have done your homework (and therefore really care about this position).

Why research?

The best thing about doing extensive research is that very few people do it, which means you'll immediately stand out from the majority of the other candidates. When asked, "Why do you want to work for us?" you will be able to impress the interviewer with your knowledge. Also, once you've conducted your research you will be well informed with regard to whether you really want to work there or not!

Regardless of what you discover, an interview is an opportunity for you to find out more and it will be in your best interest to interview well. If you don't progress to the next round, analyse what you did well and what you could improve upon, then consider it great practice for when you're applying for another role.

2. Prepare your stories and accomplishments

Read the job description thoroughly and go through all of the required skills, knowledge and competencies. Make sure that you have an example to demonstrate your capability for each of the competencies that are essential for success in the role. Review the resume you submitted, as well as your answers to the exercises in *Assess what makes you tick*. What are the tangible achievements that show that you are capable in each area, or at least have an understanding how you would approach what is required?

Your key to success is being able to link your capabilities to the company's needs. You will be hired as a solution to their problems, be it in an administrative role, a leader of change, or anything in between. Tell the story – that's what makes you real during the interview.

Review the job description and decide which of your strengths are essential for success in this role. These will be the ones that you mention when asked, "What are your key strengths?"

Beyond that, consider the common questions that come up in interviews, and prepare answers for each of them. (These don't need to be word for word, but if you have some examples you know you can touch on, you'll be less likely to get put on the spot in the interview.)

Some typical interview questions include:

- Tell me about yourself?
- Why have you applied for this role?
- What do you know about our organisation, this industry, our competitors, and our services?
- What are your relevant achievements to date?
- What work-related problems have you encountered and solved successfully?
- What examples can you provide to demonstrate your leadership ability/initiative/work ethic/effective communication skills?
- How does your past experience relate to this particular position?
- How will your skills, experience and training benefit us?
- What are your key strengths and competencies; what do you consider may be areas for improvement?
- What are your short-term and long-term career goals?

Behavioural questions

If you are in an interview with a trained interviewer, it's likely you will be asked behavioural questions. These are questions asked to get you to describe your previous behaviour in a given situation. The best predictor of future performance is past behaviour. Therefore, what you did in a similar situation in the past is likely to be repeated the next time the same or similar situation occurs.

Behavioural questions require you to demonstrate your knowledge, behaviour, or perceptions. The questions below are examples of questions that are designed to gain insight into how you think and act. Typically they cover the way you approach problem solving, the way you work within a team, your customer/client focus, adaptability, time management, organisational awareness, written communication and your motivational fit.

Typical Behavioural Questions

Analysis/problem assessment questions

- Describe a complicated problem you have had to deal with on the job. How did you identify or gain a better understanding of that problem?
- What kind of information have you been required to analyse? Describe one of your most difficult analyses.
- Have you ever had to review proposals submitted by a vendor or by another team? Tell me about one of those situations.

Teamwork/collaboration/communication skills questions

- Interacting with others can be challenging at times. Describe a situation when you wished you'd acted differently with someone at work. What happened? What did you do about the situation?
- Tell me about the manager/supervisor/team leader who was the most difficult to work for. How did you handle this difficult relationship?
- Tell me about one of the toughest teams/groups you've had to work with. What made it difficult? What did you do?
- Sometimes we have to work under new policies we don't agree with. Tell me about the last time you disagreed with a new policy or procedure instituted by senior management. Why did you disagree? What did you do?
- Can you give me an example of a team decision you were involved in recently? What did you do to help the team reach the decision?
- Sometimes it can be frustrating and trying to get information from other people so that you can solve a problem. Please describe a situation you've had like this. What did you do?

Customer service questions

- Tell me about a difficult internal/external customer you've had to deal with.
- Why was he/she difficult? What did you do?
- Describe a time when you took steps to make sure an internal/external customer was satisfied.
- Tell me about a time when you were able to respond to an internal/external customer's request in a shorter period of time than was expected. Contrast that with a time when you failed to meet an internal/external customer's expectations. What was the difference?

Planning and organising/work management questions

- We've all had times when we just couldn't get everything done on time. Tell me about a time when this has happened to you.
- Tell me about a situation when you had to adjust quickly to an organisational/departmental change or a change in team priorities. How did the change affect you?
- Has your time schedule ever been upset by unforeseen circumstances? Give me a recent example. What did you do then?
- What objectives did you set for this year? What steps have you taken to make sure you're making progress on all of them?
- At one time or another we've all forgotten to do something important for a customer. Tell me about a time this happened to you recently. What did you forget? What happened?

Organisational awareness questions

- Tell me about a recent business problem you solved. How did you utilise organisational structure (policies, systems and so on) to solve the problem?
- Sometimes you just have to disregard existing organisational policies to get something done. Tell me about a time when you knowingly disregarded an organisational policy. Why did you choose to disregard the policy? What happened?

- Give me an example of a time when you made a decision only to find out later that it was rejected. Why was it rejected? Why, do you think, was it not approved through your systems?

Written communication questions

- Tell me about one of the most important documents you have written. What reactions did it receive?
- Have you written proposals for external customers? Tell me about the best one you ever wrote. Why was it the best? How did you know that it was good?
- We've all written a memo that called for specific action only to discover later that those who received it didn't do what they were supposed to do. Can you give an example of when this happened to you?

Motivational fit questions

- When were you most satisfied/dissatisfied in your work? What was most satisfying/dissatisfying about that?
- Creativity: Tell me about a time when you were able to be creative in your work. How satisfied were you and why?
- Independence: Tell me about a time when your work was closely supervised. How satisfied were you with that and why?
- Interaction: Tell me about a time when you had many opportunities to interact with others at work. How satisfied were you with that and why?

How to respond to behavioural questions

Here's a secret for you; there is a magic solution to responding to these behavioural questions. Go back to the chapter *Assess what makes you tick* and analyse your accomplishment exercises.

By analysing the Problem, Action and Result of each of your accomplishments, you'll discover that you have used many of the behavioural traits mentioned above to achieve your positive results, though you may need to identify a few more examples of your previous accomplishments to ensure you cover each desired behaviour on the job.

Those examples will provide your responses regarding problem solving, the way you work within a team, your customer/client focus, adaptability, time management, organisational awareness, written and oral communication skills and your motivational fit. Being able to tell the story with a real example is the key to doing well as past behaviour and past successes help to determine the potential for future success.

3. Decide how you will travel to the interview and find out how long it will take

This seems obvious but, as I have experienced, some people arrive late and dishevelled to interviews because they didn't find out the best way to get to the interview location. Being late is not good. Do a Google search for the location. If you are driving, decide where will you park, and find out what the traffic will be like at that time of day.

If you are taking a bus, train or ferry, find out when the services run and how many changes will you need to make. Will you need to walk part of the way? What if it rains?

Aim to arrive 10 minutes early so that you can go to the gents or the ladies beforehand and check that you look great. This is especially important if you get caught in the rain en route to the interview. Also, this gives you time to take five long, slow deep breaths, calm yourself down, smile at yourself in the mirror and remind yourself that you are awesome and very well prepared!

4. **Make extra copies of your resume and supporting documentation**

You may be told what to bring, but I would suggest that you always have extra copies of your resume, printed on good-quality paper and in a protective folder. Have copies of your certifications and any samples of your work that might be relevant. If you aren't asked for them, that won't be a problem; however, if they ask you and you don't have them, it will show that you are not prepared.

Bring a pen and a small notepad with you in case you need to take notes at any stage. I don't recommending taking notes during an interview, as it will be distracting to the interviewer. However, it's good to have them with you just in case, as each interview will present different opportunities.

5. **Decide what you will wear to the interview**

Review the chapter *Express your professional image* to be sure that you are appropriately dressed. As part of your research you must find out how people typically dress in the department where you hope to work. Then decide to dress one notch up from that to show that this interview matters to you.

I coached a marketing candidate back in 2002 who was going for a marketing manager role at a very trendy telecommunications company that had a reputation for innovation, creativity and fun.

He was only 29 years old and yet, when we went through interview practice (I'd asked him to wear what he planned to wear to the interview), he turned up in a black suit, white shirt and black tie. I asked him, "Who died?" (It just blurted out of my mouth before I could stop myself.) I was concerned and told him that the 'look' was not trendy, creative or fun. However, he said it was his interview suit and he didn't want to change it. Luckily, the interview he went to was with a recruitment consultant with a heart.

He called me after the interview to debrief and he told me that the first thing she said to him was, "Lighten up and don't wear a black tie!" He toned down the severe look; at the next interview, he wore a charcoal grey suit with a light shirt and a deep golden yellow tie.

This still looked professional and the yellow conveyed intellect, energy, confidence and positivity. This worked well for him, I believe, because of the emotional response that colour can evoke in others. Yellow has been used as the 'first' for many things in business, like the Post-it note and the highlighter because it gets your attention faster than any other colour. In this case, yellow was a good choice for a role that required an innovative approach.

6. Practise positive body language

An open stance, warm smile, good eye contact and firm handshake are all essential to convey confidence and professionalism. The first impression is so important as it paves the way for a smoother interview. For more details on body language, flip back to *Express your professional image*.

7. Relax!

Once you are well prepared you can give yourself a pat on the back and then relax so that you are feeling fresh and looking forward to the interview.

To help you stay calm, ensure you are maintaining a healthy lifestyle – eat a balanced diet, exercise to manage your stress levels and get enough sleep. Have another read through the techniques for managing stress in *Confidently manage change* as a reminder of all the steps you can take to maintain confidence in yourself and handle challenges. You want to walk into the interview as the best version of YOU that you can be. If you're tired, stressed, rushed or unwell, the first impression you give won't be your best. At an interview, the person across the table will perceive that this is as good as it gets!

> **Mark's Story**
>
> Recently Mark had taken on a part-time evening role to bring in some money while looking for a permanent full-time role as a business analyst. The evening role was a manual labour late shift at his wife's place of business and during the days he had taken on the responsibility of doing the school runs and housework as well as looking for a job.
>
> Consequently, he was not getting enough sleep and I was concerned as, at each of our coaching sessions, he looked exhausted, had extremely dark circles under his eyes and was lacking in energy. He was not the best version of himself – he found it difficult to concentrate during our sessions and found that, due to exhaustion, he was reacting more emotionally than was normal.
>
> We discussed managing his time and looking after his health so he could present himself at his best in interviews. This resulted in him asking for help from other family members so that he could get enough essential rest and within two weeks he'd sorted out a schedule with his family and friends. He looked much fresher at our meetings, had more energy to put into the job search and was able to focus. Health comes first. You can't do anything well if you don't take care of yourself.

What to do during the interview

Before you get all worked up about the interview, just remember that the most important thing in an interview is to demonstrate that you are the right person for the job.

In order to do that, keep the following in mind:
- Do you know your audience? As part of your preparation you will have looked them up on LinkedIn as well as getting in touch

with any mutual contacts who can provide additional insights. Based on your research, what is most important to the hiring manager, and how can you meet that need?

- Chemistry counts for a lot – good managers and executives learn to trust their gut instincts as well as consider what's in your resume. Be genuine, be open and relax. Look the hiring manager in the eye, smile. Make a connection.
- Do you meet the job specifications? What are the functional requirements of the role and what are the soft skills required (communication skills, personal characteristics, influencing skills and so on) and what are your examples to show your command of these?
- Are you being true to yourself? Are you representing yourself accurately? Make sure you are as good as your resume says, otherwise there will be major disappointment on both sides.
- What is your experience and can you talk about it? It doesn't always matter how many years you have been performing a specific task, it's the results you've achieved that count. Make sure you can tell the story, using the Problem – Action – Result methodology. Relate how you did it, the challenges, how you overcame them, the results and what you learnt.
- How do you approach problem solving? Do you have examples of your street smarts? Be aware that you may be asked some unusual questions seemingly unrelated to the job too. Recently one of my clients, Peter, told me, "I was thrown a curve ball and was asked what I'd do if given a million dollars. I think the hiring manager wanted to know if I could think on my feet as it would have been unlikely that I'd have prepared for that specific question. Luckily I had an answer as my distant BHAG (Big Hairy Audacious Goal) is to buy a coffee shop in the CBD and provide training and employment for the long-term unemployed." He said the interviewer told him it was a great response and I was impressed that he had a vision and was able to demonstrate his passion with such ease.

- What is it like to be in your presence? What's your personality? Are you laid back, are you a go-getter, do you have a strong sense of entitlement or do you have an exceptional work ethic? Are you driven? Are you grounded? How do you handle responsibility? Understand yourself. The exercises in *Assess what makes you tick* prepare you for this.
- Are you a team player or more insular? What type of person is required for the role? Be aware of how you may fit in this environment.
- Are you like-minded? Look out for clues as to the preferred communication style of the hiring manager. Be open-minded so you can learn from each other and, if the connection is there, you have a greater chance of success.

The other thing to keep in mind is what the interviewer is looking for. Imagine you are interviewing someone to replace you. What would you be looking for? Would the following questions be on your mind?

- Can this candidate do the job and does he/she have the necessary qualifications or certifications?
- How much enthusiasm does this candidate have for our company?
- How long will this candidate stay with us; is this role his/her dream job or is it just an interim measure?
- Will we respect each other; will this candidate fit in with the team?
- How motivated is this candidate to perform this role and perhaps exceed expectations?
- Can I rely on this candidate?
- Will this candidate work the way we need him/her to (part-time/full-time/flexitime/interstate or international travel/accept late night international conference calls, etc.)?
- What salary would this candidate expect?

Remember that the interviewer may be thinking these things, even if he or she doesn't specifically ask, so focus on how you can put the interviewer at ease about how serious you are about this role; how you can express your enthusiasm, passion, and drive to succeed; how you can show you'll be a valuable team member or leader; and how you can demonstrate your integrity and work ethic.

So much of this is expressed through words and, as discussed in *Express your professional image*, your tone of voice and body language.

Be aware of your body language

Remember the importance of first impressions and keep an eye on your body language.

- Sit or face the person squarely.
- Adopt an open posture. (Don't cross your arms!)
- Lean forward slightly – this helps show your interest and attentiveness.
- Indicate with verbal comments that you are following what the other person is saying.
- Make eye contact.
- Relax.

Questions to ask during the interview

I find my clients tend to overlook the questions that they can ask during an interview. Remember that an interview is a two-way street. The interviewer wants to learn about you and YOU want to learn about the position and the environment that you will be working in.

If you were to be offered the role, then you start in the job and realise that it's not a good fit for you, whose fault would it be? Yours, because you accepted it without asking the questions you needed to ask to make the informed decision to take the role or not.

Also, if the hiring manager asks you at the end of the interview, "So, do you have any questions for me?" and you answer, "No" then you have committed a fatal error by demonstrating that you have not prepared yourself as well as you could have. It will demonstrate that you haven't done your homework, and that you don't care about doing that little bit extra for this particular role. By not asking questions to really understand every aspect of the role, you are missing a very important opportunity to REALLY sell yourself.

Think about these questions and what you would think if you were the interviewer and a potential candidate asked them:

- If I were to be offered the role and I started tomorrow, what would be the top priority in my 'to do' list?
- What are the key qualities of the successful candidate in this role?
- What improvements do you hope the successful candidate will make in this role?
- What is the most important aspect of your corporate culture?
- Are there any concerns that you may have about my capabilities that are not quite a match for this role?
- How do you measure success in this role?
- What could I do to exceed expectations in this role?
- What is it that excited you about joining this company?
- What are the qualities that the top-performing employees possess here?
- What do you hope the successful candidate will achieve in the first 90 days of taking on this role?

These questions give you an additional insight into the actual requirements of a successful candidate in the role. These questions show that you are really interested in what works in this workplace and their expectations. In short, by asking the right questions, you are positioning yourself for success.

Inappropriate questions

Sometimes an interviewer may ask questions that verge on being inappropriate, such as:

- How old are you?
- What church do you attend?
- How many children do you have?
- Do you plan to get married in the near future?
- Do you plan to have children in the near future?
- What kind of accent is that?

How you respond to these questions is up to you in the privacy of an interview room; however, if a question makes you feel uncomfortable you could simply respond by asking how this has any bearing on your ability to perform in the role. If you feel even more strongly, I would suggest excusing yourself politely and leaving by saying, "It was a pleasure meeting you. If you have questions about my ability to perform in this role I'd be more than happy to answer them in a follow-up meeting. Thank you for your time." Remember that if a workplace does not feel right to you during the interview, it's unlikely to feel better later on. The choice is yours.

A note about the salary question

While not an inappropriate question, questions about salary can make a lot of us feel uncomfortable.

If you are asked about your salary expectations, tell the interviewer that you'd like to know more about the role first so that you can more accurately gauge what you'd expect to earn in that role.

Avoid divulging your last salary if possible, unless the role is at a very similar level in a similar-sized company in a similar industry in the same city. You need to be sure that, when it comes to salary expectations, you are comparing apples with apples, not apples with shallots.

One way to do this is by researching the latest salary surveys. There are numerous salary surveys available online. Here are a few sites where you can download the latest salary surveys as a comparison:

- www.robertwalters.com.au
- www.michaelpage.com.au
- www.seek.com.au

In your interview, focus on the salary range that you believe you're realistically worth based on your research, skills and experience. This may be a different figure from what you were earning in your last job.

If asked what your last salary package was and you feel you must answer this without deflecting, let them know, with the caveat that your salary expectation for the role you're being interviewed for will depend on the scope and responsibilities of the role.

In any case, do not lie about your previous or current salary! Be honest, because you don't want to start a job only to have the truth emerge that compromises your credibility.

What types of interviews might you encounter?

Screening interviews

This is usually done over the phone once the initial review of resumes is over. A certain number of the top candidate resumes are chosen and if yours is one of them you will be called.

If you've made a number of applications it would be reasonable to expect at least one screening call at some stage in the process.

Make sure that you are prepared to handle a screening call as it can happen at any time of day; when you are in the office, at the gym, at the shopping centre, walking down the street, at lunch ... you get my point.

Remember that you must have your verbal pitch fresh in your mind at all times. When I was in recruitment and I'd call candidates who looked good on paper, it was really off-putting when I couldn't hear them properly, they didn't explain themselves clearly and didn't even know the role they'd applied for! All they needed to do was to find somewhere quiet to speak and sound professional. As professionalism was a key behaviour I was listening out for, those who were poorly prepared did not get past that first phone call.

The key to success here is to be clear, accurate and concise in your delivery of what you have to offer that's relevant to the role. This screening is to ensure that you have the qualifications to perform the role and also to determine if you have any obvious qualities or characteristics that might prevent you from being successful in the role.

This means that, if you get a call from a screener when it is not convenient for you to speak, or it's too noisy to be heard, ask if it would be all right for you to call back and GET THEIR NAME AND CONTACT DETAILS! Don't ask them to call you back as they probably won't. A screener has a number of calls to make and if other candidates are subsequently screened and are suitable, you might not get a call back. Keep the ball in your court and, as soon as you are able, make that call yourself.

If you are able to speak, listen carefully to the questions and respond accordingly. The screening interview is not usually the time when you go into great detail, unless you are asked. Make it easy for the screener to find out that you possess the basics of what they need. You may then be called in for a skills test, or asked to complete one online if that is required for the role you are targeting.

The initial screening is designed to confirm some of what is in your resume and cover letter and to determine if you speak well enough to be understood. (There are very few roles that don't require good verbal communication skills.)

If the call is successful and you are told you will be contacted again for the next step, still ask for their contact details. If you don't hear back after a few days you should follow up yourself.

Skype/video/webcam interviews

There may be times when the interviewer is in another state or country. If this is the case you will be given a time (and where to go) to attend a remote interview.

Treat this as if it were a face-to-face interview. Dress appropriately for the occasion and avoid any obvious patterns in your shirt or blouse in case they are distracting. You want the interviewer to focus on your face and what you have to say.

If you are to be called at home for the interview, make sure that you are in a quiet place. Put the dog out of earshot for the time being and, if you have young children or a baby at home, have someone mind them (also out of earshot) while you are in the interview. It's important that you focus and create as professional an environment as possible.

If you are not familiar with using Skype or looking into a webcam, please practise on a friend beforehand so you are comfortable with the technology. In order to look natural and make what feels like eye contact, you need to look at the camera on the computer and not at the screen. When you look at the screen it appears to the viewer that you are looking downwards.

My private coaching clients contact me via Skype or FaceTime and I always have a contingency plan just in case we have technical difficulties. If I experience a problem on the computer and need to restart, I will call them on either a landline or mobile to continue the conversation.

Make sure you turn off your email updates, your mobile, and anything else that pops up with alerts that could be distracting.

As you would during a face-to-face interview, have a copy of the version of the resume you submitted with you and any other information that you might need on hand. Be prepared and you will present yourself well.

Panel interviews

Panel interviews can be a little nerve wracking, especially if you were not expecting a panel interview and you walk into the room to find there's not one pair of eyes watching you but two, three, four or more! The good thing is that you are usually told in advance if it is to be a panel interview, so there is time to get your head around it.

Panel interviews are beneficial for the employer, being time-effective and giving multiple stakeholders the chance to consider how well you'll fit into the organisation. Often team members/peers will be included in a panel interview, as they will be the ones who will be working with you if you are successful – remember, chemistry and fit are of utmost importance when you join a team.

Panels also give these stakeholders the chance to understand what you have to offer and explain to you how things will work if you get the job. This provides you with the opportunity to understand how the role fits within the organisational structure.

Finally, by increasing the pressure, a panel interview gives the interviewers an indication as to how you will react under pressure with those in authority and those within the team.

If you are given a heads up as to who will be in the interview, you can prepare by researching each individual. When conducting research, this is a time when you might wish to have your profile show up in the 'Who's viewed your profile' section on LinkedIn. Each interviewer will know that you've done your due diligence when preparing for the interview if they see that you've viewed their profile beforehand.

However, if you've been told that John, Tony and Peter will be interviewing you, don't be surprised if Ken has replaced Peter at the last minute because something came up. Be prepared for any changes and remain adaptable at all times. Of course you will have brought extra copies of your resume with you just in case a few more people drop in! If you have your notepad and pen with you, make sure you write down everyone's names so you don't forget.

My clients tell me the hardest thing during a panel interview is knowing where to look when responding to interviewers and how to gauge who the key decision maker will be. What I recommend is to treat all the attendees with equal respect, as they are there for a good reason and a panel will reduce the level of bias that one interviewer may have towards you.

When one of the panel members asks you a question, start your answer by addressing that person first and then include the others with your eye contact. Speaking clearly is of vital importance and directing your gaze at each person will include them in your answer, even if one or two of them are looking down jotting notes as you speak.

When they wind up the interview, thank them and offer to shake each person's hand. A firm handshake, eye contact and warm smile while thanking them for their time and letting them know you look forward to continuing discussions is a good way to end on a positive note.

One-on-one interviews

After worrying about the panel interview, the prospect of an interview with just one person will seem like a relief! This is the traditional method for interviewing, which can be conducted by a recruitment consultant, an internal recruiter or the person who may be your direct manager.

As with panel interviews, offering a firm handshake upon meeting the interviewer, maintaining good eye contact and giving a warm, genuine smile are all ways to start off on a positive note. The same applies when leaving the interview.

The interviewer will be looking for a specific set of skills and aptitudes for the role. What you want to do is present yourself confidently and professionally by being well-prepared, having excellent examples of your past accomplishments ready and being ready to ask additional questions when given the chance, to ensure that you fully understand the requirements of the role.

Peter Bouris, Head of IT&T at Lloyd Harrington, one of Australia's leading recruitment agencies, explains that in a typical interview: "We review and question parts of the resume that require confirmation and clarification, question the candidate around the specific requirements of the role and then provide time for the interviewee to ask questions. At the end of each interview we clarify the next steps and the timeline for each step."

Sequential interviews

You may be asked to complete an interview with one person and then go and meet one more or several more who are part of the selection process. This could happen on the same day or over the course of a few days (or weeks, in some cases). If this should happen, make sure that you maintain the same energy level at each subsequent meeting. Don't assume that each interviewer will have had time to compare notes before meeting you. Treat each meeting as your first meeting, as you will, very likely, be asked the same questions several times by each individual.

If you are told in advance of this process, conduct research on each person you will meet!

What to do after the interview

You walk out of the interview and think, "Phew! I'm glad that's over!" What do you do next?

Do you ever follow up after your interviews? Or do you simply wait and hope?

When I was working in recruitment, I was amazed at the number of people who failed to continue to sell themselves effectively by providing a thank you email after their interviews. They must have thought, *I did all I could do during the interview, now I can sit back and relax.* No, no, no – there is more to be done!

Take notes immediately after the interview

After you leave the interview, I suggest that you go somewhere comfortable, sit down and, while everything is fresh in your memory, write down what transpired.

Take note of the date and time, everyone you met, the tone of the interview, the focus of the questions, what went well and what didn't go so well. Write down what the interviewer/s said were the next steps so you know when to follow up if you don't hear back from them.

If a recruitment consultant organised the interview, give them a call to debrief and provide feedback on your take on how things went. They will also want to know if, after the interview, you are still interested in the role.

Send a thank you email

Craft an effective thank you email to the interviewer as a follow-up. This shows them that you're able to take the initiative to do something above and beyond the norm, and, by taking the extra step that many candidates don't, you continue to set yourself apart. This will demonstrate your attention to detail, provide an effective finishing touch to the interview and give you one more opportunity to sell your qualifications and relevant experience (according to your analysis of the interview). This will also provide an opportunity to demonstrate your gratitude for being considered, your continued interest in the role, and leave a positive impression on the reader. Finally, it's just a thoughtful thing to do.

You should send the thank you email as soon as possible after the interview. If you don't have the interviewer's business card, do some research to find out their email address. If you are working through a recruiter, ask the recruiter if it would be all right for you to send an email to the interviewer. The recruiter may prefer you to send the email to him or her and then your email will be forwarded on your behalf.

What should go into a follow-up email? It's simple to remember the four Rs:

> R - Remember me (and get your name noticed one more time!)
> R - Reinforce the positives
> R - Recoup your losses
> R - Remind both parties of the next steps

For example:

> Dear (Name),
>
> It was my pleasure to meet with you today to discuss the role of XYZ at (company name).
>
> I was most interested to find out about (key highlights of the interview most relevant to performing successfully in the role) as my experience/knowledge/skills in (mention what's most important) are a close match to your requirements.
>
> With regard to (what you felt you could have answered more strongly) my time/my experience/my skills/my abilities in (what they need) place me in a strong position to get up to speed with ease.
>
> As mentioned during the interview, I look forward to hearing from you by (date) and to continuing discussions. If I may provide any additional information you require, please let me know.
>
> I look forward to hearing from you. Best wishes,
>
> Your name

This puts your name in front of the interviewer one more time. The first paragraph gives you the opportunity to express your enthusiasm and reinforce all your positives that are a match to the role, the next paragraph gives you a chance to redeem yourself if you totally messed up a response, as you can mention your capability in that specific area of concern and, in the final paragraph, if you were given a date by when you might hear back, mention that you are looking forward to discussing this position further after that date.

Then remember to proofread before sending!

What if you are turned down for the role?

If you are turned down, don't burn bridges. Send another thank you email. Let the employer know that you appreciate that you were considered for the role, that their company is still your company of choice and if, in the future, suitable positions arise, you would be delighted to be considered again. This will keep channels of communication open. The preferred candidate might not make it through the probationary period and then YOU could be their back-up plan if you are still available and interested in the position.

In fact, I have a six-week rule where you make contact with the decision maker one more time six weeks after the preferred candidate has started in the role. When you make contact, it's just to keep in touch with something of value. Perhaps it's a white paper with interesting research on your area of expertise or it's a link to an article that will be of interest to the manager. This extra contact is another touch point that can keep the relationship warm. As I said before, don't burn bridges.

As an example of how following up can lead to success, here's a comment I received from a woman who read one of my LinkedIn published articles about following up:

She wrote, *"I recently shifted career directions and had a promising interview for a long-term contract position. They emailed to let me know that I was not selected and I chose to follow up to request feedback on how I could make myself a stronger candidate for future similar opportunities.*

"She got right back to me and explained that they went with someone with more direct experience but also asked me if I might be interested in another shorter-term contract position. I was offered that role, which ended up being extended far past the role that I initially interviewed for.

"Furthermore, it allowed me to do work based on my strengths and accomplish some things that I had never anticipated being able to

do in such a short amount of time! I always wonder if she would have thrown that opportunity out to me had I not rather cheekily asked her for feedback."

What will tip the balance for you in an interview?

Now that you've gone through what to expect and what to do before, during and after an interview, you should feel a little more comfortable about your chances of success.

However, just reading the information in this chapter is not going to make you as prepared as you need to be. Review your examples and your successes and work them into each of your responses where appropriate.

Practise out loud, not just in your head — and practise in front of a mirror. I do this before every presentation I conduct. I used to feel a bit silly doing that but I soon got used to it as I started to adapt my expressions, my tonal inflections for greater impact and my body language. You can even record yourself using a mobile device or a recorder if that helps. Analyse yourself. Do you impress yourself? If not, then practise until you are able to look yourself in the mirror and say to yourself, "You've nailed it!"

Do your research, read between the lines, and think about something unique that you could bring to the role. You will be way ahead of the competition. The key to interview success? Preparation!

Visit THE CAREERS ACADEMY ONLINE www.thecareersacademy.online for more support on interview preparation and career management.

SUCCESS STRATEGIES IN YOUR NEW ROLE

"Don't bargain yourself down before you get to the table."

Carol Frohlinger, Managing Director of Negotiating Women, Inc.

Congratulations, you've been offered the job! This is exciting and you will definitely feel a little lightheaded when you are told, "We'd like to offer you the role!"

Before you say, "Yes!" it's a good idea to consider a few things first. Here are some suggestions.

First of all, you don't have to give an answer right away. Your adrenaline levels will probably be quite high when you hear those magic words and you want to be sure that you fully understand the terms of the offer before you accept. That means you need time to go over the paperwork.

What you hear when you are in an elevated sense of excitement may be different from what is actually being said. Let's not be too hasty unless it's such an amazing offer that you can't refuse!

So, when you are offered the role, express your thanks and enthusiasm for the role. Say that you are looking forward to adding value in this role and you are keen to go through the letter of offer and contract so you fully understand the terms of employment.

You will always have at least 24 hours to consider the offer. Many of my clients like to discuss the offer with their partners or family before accepting or rejecting an offer, as the decision will affect them too.

When the letter of offer and/or contract is sent to you (this will come via courier, post or email), go through each item with a critical eye. If you decide to negotiate on the offer, and you were originally put forward for the role by a recruitment consultant then they will offer to do the negotiation on your behalf. You must be sure to let the consultant know what is and what is not acceptable to you. They will then advise you through the process.

If you are conducting the negotiations yourself, ensure you prepare so you can negotiate from a position of strength. You must have clear and realistic expectations of what your skills and experience are worth and be prepared to ask your potential employer for what you want.

Determine your needs

Most of my clients are keen to just discuss the salary when we go over negotiation strategies together when, in fact, what needs to be considered are all aspects of the role before you pin a number on what would be acceptable to you.

Go through all of the tangible factors of the offer: salary, bonuses, package, perks, industry, job function, working hours, flexibility, promotional prospects and so on.

Go through all of the intangible factors for your job satisfaction: corporate culture, team environment, work environment, opportunities for advancement, type of manager and so on.

How does the offer and everything that you have learned about the company, the role, the people and the salary package compare with your dream job? Are your 'Must haves' covered? If not, are you still considering accepting the role? If so, what is your reasoning?

By making this comparison you will see instantly where there are areas that you may wish to discuss during the negotiation process. If the offer doesn't quite stack up for you, it's time to strategise what you're going to do about it.

Let's think about the salary for now. Determine a realistic salary range for negotiation. Think about the following:

- What you need to live on comfortably
- What you would be satisfied with (the absolute minimum you would accept, with everything else considered)
- What you would be delighted with (a realistic ultimate goal)
- Current market rate

The absolute minimum salary acceptable to you and your ultimate goal, while keeping in mind the current market rate, is the salary range that you should have in your head. You can start negotiations at the higher end to allow room for discussion.

Know what you are worth

Arm yourself with the facts. You won't benefit by bargaining from ignorance. Check out websites such as glassdoor.com and recruitment agency websites like www.robertwalters.com for their salary surveys as they'll give you an idea of what the current market rate is in your city, your industry and at your level within this size of organisation.

Scan similar jobs on the Internet as some job advertisements provide a salary range as a guide. Talk to industry colleagues for advice on what people are earning in similar positions.

Research company conditions

Make sure you also research the financial performance of the company, its recent staff movements and industry conditions. You can look at www.avention.com/onesource for this information. If you don't have a subscription to the service, check with your local library, as you may be able to gain access to their databases by joining the library. Also check out www.glassdoor.com again as you can gain company information here too. This will help you to understand the company's position and anticipate potential objections when negotiating your salary.

Watch your timing

The time to negotiate is AFTER you have received the offer, not before. You are in the strongest position to negotiate salary when the employer has offered you the role, is hopeful of employing you and has a suggested package for you.

Consider other options

A good negotiator will enter a meeting with a range of options. When deciding on how you will approach the negotiation process, if you believe that the opportunity to negotiate the salary is limited, think about non-pay alternatives. Flexible working arrangements, support for education and training are potential alternatives to financial incentives. If the job offers a clear promotion path or the opportunity to review your salary in three to six months, this may help you to decide what is and what is not acceptable right now. If the probationary period is six months, you might suggest reducing it to three months if you were to meet the KPIs within that time frame. You could also suggest a sign-on bonus if the base salary is not negotiable. Make sure you consider all alternatives as part of your negotiations.

Make it a win-win

Employers respect applicants who know their worth and are not afraid to have the discussion. Having the confidence to negotiate well for yourself shows the employer that you could bring these skills to the role and this will strengthen their belief that you are a valuable addition to their team. Don't fear presenting a counter to their offer. It's expected and demonstrates a healthy sense of self-worth.

During the negotiation process, remain calm. Your energy and enthusiasm must come through, not anxiety and desperation! Make sure you get it right from the start with your expectations. It's not normally possible to correct flawed negotiations in your next performance review. It's important to keep in mind that negotiation is about knowing what you want, going after it, and respecting the other person in the process. The point of negotiating is to reach a compromise that is acceptable to both you and the company.

How to open negotiations

Once you've gone over the documentation and have decided on what you'd like to negotiate and what your walk-away point will be, then you are ready to pick up the phone. Don't make that call until you are clear about what is most important to you.

If you will not take the role as it stands, mentally take yourself through the process of what you will say if you are told there is no room for negotiation. If you can't take the role as it stands then you will have to respectfully decline their offer.

Don't bluff – we are looking for a situation where both parties will be happy; we are not going in to battle where only one of you will win. You want to be adequately compensated for a job well done and the employer will want value for their investment.

When you have the relevant party on the phone, express again your enthusiasm for the role and ask if there is room for discussion on the package. If there is, they will ask what you would like to discuss. If possible, ask for a face-to-face meeting to discuss, as negotiations are best when you can read the other person's body language. If they prefer to discuss immediately, you will be prepared so, open negotiations.

When you open negotiations, ask for what is most important to you first. Everything else will be a bonus if you get it. If you start with the lesser items on your agenda, you may find that after a few 'yes' outcomes it will be harder to gain another 'yes' when it comes to your final and most important discussion point.

What about multiple job offers or an offer from your second choice?

I've received a number of panicked phone calls from clients who have received an offer from their second choice of role while they are still waiting for the next step of the selection process from their first choice.

Under such circumstances you should contact your preferred employer and ask if you are in serious consideration for the role as you have been made an offer and you must give your answer by a certain date.

If the selection process is far enough along that they don't want to lose you, you may find that they will speed things up. If it is too early for them to determine, then the final call is up to you.

Let your preferred employer know that they are your first choice; however, you now need to make a decision. If you decide to take your 2nd choice role, don't burn bridges, and respectfully let them know that you would like to remain in contact with them should circumstances change in the future.

And remember, you don't have to make the decision alone – discuss it with someone you respect, who understands you, and also has a good understanding of your particular market. Armed with relevant information, and by following your gut feelings, you will have the courage to make the right decision. Of course you don't have to negotiate, but if you decide to, I hope that some of these suggestions will be helpful to you!

On-boarding into the new role

Congratulations on negotiating well and accepting an offer that is a win-win. Now you have a start date! I'm thinking champagne celebrations and big, big smiles all around! (My clients know how excited I get for them when they reach this stage.)

If you've been offered a role and can't wait to start, email jane@janejacksoncoach.com and ask to join my *Career Crossroads Community Forum* and share the joy! Our community will be delighted for you and your success will be a huge motivator for the others still going through the marketing and interviewing processes.

So now what? If you've got time, take a little break, relax, enjoy and recharge your batteries before starting the new role. Get all your paperwork in order, clear the clutter in your home environment, have the coffee catch-ups and lunches or dinners to celebrate and prepare yourself mentally for the exciting new challenges ahead!

Most large organisations have on-boarding processes to help you to transition smoothly into your new role. Each process can vary greatly from a quick tour and introduction to team members to a week-long (or longer) on-boarding process for you to become familiarised with the systems, personnel and location. The first 90 days in this new role are crucial for your reputation and also your self-esteem.

Give yourself a head start by starting the process yourself. Here are my eight steps to on-boarding success:

1. **The first steps to success in a new job begin before the first day.** Once you've accepted the role, contact the hiring manager and your human resources contact. Let them know you are looking forward to getting on board and convey your enthusiasm for the new role.
2. **Connect on LinkedIn with those you've met during the selection process.** Make sure your profile is as strong as it can be as others within your team will probably check out your profile before you turn up on your first day.
3. **Create a 30-, 60- and 90-day plan with your new manager.** This will give you a map to follow during your initiation into the company and the expectations of your role. Having measurable benchmarks developed with the organisation's business goals in mind will help you greatly with clear direction. Ensure you understand how your success will be measured so you will know where to focus your attention initially and in the longer term.
4. **Identify the resources you need to do your job early on.** This will be anything from office supplies, phone and mobile connection to the technology required to get things done. Get to know the administration and technical support team as you will need them! There are always individuals within any company who can help you get things done because of their workplace knowledge or their relationships with key people within the organisation. Find out who those people are and develop a relationship with them as they will be the people who can help when you are stuck.
5. **Look for ways to make a difference even in the early days.** Of course it's important to develop good working relationships very early on; however, while you are doing so, see where you can pick the low hanging fruit and get some wins on the board.

After the first 30 days it will be time to demonstrate the value that you bring.

6. **Always show respect for the people and events that have come before you.** It's wise to ask questions that show appreciation for current employees and respect for those who came before you. Be very tactful, especially in the early days, even if you believe you completely understand the political landscape of the organisation. You won't really know who's who in the zoo until you've been there a while.
7. **Check in with your manager every week or two to make sure you are on track.** As you learn more from your stakeholders you will be able to manage expectations. Always be willing to ask for your manager's help if you need it.
8. **Stay positive.** There will be good days, better days and some days when you may feel a little disappointed. The first couple of weeks will see you transitioning from excitement about the new role to the reality of the day-to-day routine and challenges. Displaying energy and enthusiasm for the role will benefit your reputation amongst your colleagues. A new role can be quite stressful, so give yourself time to settle in and know that no one is perfect. Make the effort to understand the way things work and always be willing to ask questions and listen to the answers.

Whether you're changing roles within an organisation or joining a new one, you will need to learn new skills for success.

As Professor Sattar Bawany, CEO and Master Executive Coach, Centre for Executive Education says, "Executives in a new role confront the need to adapt to new business models and organisational cultures, and to build supportive networks. The biggest trap they may fall into is to believe they will continue to be successful by doing what has made them successful in the past.

There is an old saying: *'To a person who has a hammer, everything looks like a nail.'* New leaders must focus first on discovering what it will take to be successful in the new role, then discipline themselves to do the things that don't come naturally if the situation demands it."

However don't let this overwhelm you – look forward to your first 90 days confident in the knowledge that you will settle in comfortably once you know how things work in your new environment while keeping an open, flexible and positive attitude. I wish you much success and a fabulous new career ahead!

CONCLUSION

"Happiness is a direction, not a place."

– Sydney J. Harris

We've now come to the end of Navigating Career Crossroads, but this is only the beginning for you. Keep referring back to the relevant sections in this CAREERS programme for ongoing guidance to enable you to navigate your career crossroads.

I sincerely hope that all the suggestions, practical exercises, relaxation techniques, professional image management and job search tools will give you the momentum to take control of your career with confidence, courage and clarity. By following this process you will:

1. Feel worthy and of value, confident of your capabilities and able to handle the multiple changes in your life
2. Discover your passion, and feel confident about your new direction, clear on what you are capable of
3. Be well prepared to launch your marketing campaign, to expand your network and interview effectively to secure the career of your dreams

I hope this book leaves you feeling absolute belief in yourself, courageous and confident.

I believe that anyone who lacks confidence, passion and direction is capable of rediscovering the person they forgot they are. We're all born into this world kicking and screaming with confidence –

expecting attention, expecting to be fed, expecting to be looked after and loved – because we're all worth it.

This means you, too, have the opportunity to be happy, to feel fulfilled, and to live with passion and direction. There has never been a better time in your life than now to take action!

Always remember, *"Magic is believing in yourself. If you can do that, you can make anything happen." – Johann Wolfgang von Goethe*

For ongoing support, join me in THE CAREERS ACADEMY ONLINE where monthly group coaching sessions via Zoom video conferencing is included, PLUS I offer a 30-minute one-on-one coaching session with me at no charge, included in a low monthly membership.

I look forward to having you join our Careers Academy community for coaching support, resources and peer support too! www.thecareersacademy.online

To keep you on track to reach your goals, join my GET STUFF DONE Facebook Accountability private group: www.facebook.com/groups/getstuffdoneaccountability

RESOURCES

Access all my career resources and links for selected recruitment agencies, career coaching and support, leadership and executive coaching, job boards, volunteering, and internship information: www.janejacksoncoach.com/resources

WITH GRATITUDE

I am so grateful to have the opportunity to write a book on a topic for which I have such passion. There are so many wonderful people I must thank for assisting me along this journey.

First of all, thank you to my family. To my incredible husband, Tony, without whose love, humour and emotional support this book would not have been possible. To my amazing daughters, Jess and Jo, who are my ongoing inspiration; a source of joy, love and delight. To my brother, Tom, for your support and my warm and wonderful extended family, Susan, Kate, Nick, Hayley, Timmy, Marc, Vasilli, Mark and Hannah. To all my girlfriends whose unconditional love and support has always kept me on track.

Thank you to my wonderful clients and colleagues who shared so freely of their experiences and advice in this book. This book is all the more valuable because you are in it.

To Andrew Griffiths, author and mentor extraordinaire, without whose encouragement and advice this book would have been just a pipe dream, and the amazing KPI team for ongoing 'aha' moments.

A huge thanks to my talented editor, Jacqueline Pretty from Grammar Factory, and my book designer, Helen Christie. My gratitude to my publishing genius Andrew Akratos, from OMNE, for your support, professionalism and all round 'awesomeness' in getting stuff done. Nothing is ever too much trouble – you are amazing!

And finally, a very special thank you to every career coach I am blessed to work alongside – you know who you are!

Warmest wishes,

Jane x

CPSIA information can be obtained
at www.ICGtesting.com
Printed in the USA
LVHW031101020223
738487LV00004B/75